A CHRONOLOGY OF THE WORKS OF GUILLAUME DUFAY

NUMBER ONE IN THE PRINCETON STUDIES IN MUSIC

A Chronology of the Works

of

Guillaume Dufay

Based on a Study of

Mensural Practice

BY

CHARLES E. HAMM

1964

PRINCETON UNIVERSITY PRESS

PRINCETON, NEW JERSEY

Copyright © 1964 by Princeton University Press
ALL RIGHTS RESERVED
L.C. Card 63-9992

Publication of this book has been aided by the
Whitney Darrow Publication Reserve Fund of
Princeton University Press and by the aid of the
Elsie and Walter W. Naumburg Fund in the
Department of Music, Princeton University.

Part of Chapter Five of this study appeared as
"Dating a Group of Dufay Works," in *JAMS*,
vol. 15 (1962, pp. 65-71).

Second Printing, with corrections, 1967

Printed in the United States of America
by Murray Printing Company

TO

ARTHUR MENDEL

*who directed and encouraged me
in this study from its beginning*

PREFACE

The notation of the music of the first half of the fifteenth century has never been studied in detail.

Basic principles of this notational system are relatively simple and are understood well enough today. The manuals of Wolf[1] and Tirabassi,[2] and the more recent one by Apel,[3] explain these principles in more or less clear fashion, and with their help a student can learn to transcribe almost any piece from the period. Difficulties arise only when there are errors in the manuscript, or when the composer or scribe has not understood details of mensural notation as well as the student himself.

But it is possible that a more detailed study of certain features of this notation would yield valuable information. If notational practice changed during this period and the changes could be detected, rationalized, and proven to have a chronological ordering, they could be used to date entire groups of compositions. If differences in notational practice could be detected among the works of various composers, no matter how slight and apparently insignificant the differences might be, they could help in the attribution of anonymous and dubious works to specific composers.

Various details of the notation could be taken as a point of departure for such a study. It has been suggested, for example, that a close study of ligature usage might be fruitful. But a preliminary study convinced me that valuable results could be obtained from an investigation of the different mensurations used and the signatures employed at times to specify these mensurations.[4] I conceived of the plan of setting up a chronological outline of mensural practice against which any composition could

[1] Johannes Wolf, Geschichte der Mensural-Notation von 1250-1460 (Leipzig, 1904).

[2] A. Tirabassi, Grammaire de la notation proportionnelle et sa transcription moderne (Brussels, 1928).

[3] Willi Apel, The Notation of Polyphonic Music 900-1600 (Cambridge, 1953).

[4] I will use the term "mensuration" when speaking of the organization of a piece (i.e., the number of semibreves per breve, the number of minims per semibreve, etc.) and the term "signature" when speaking of the symbol used to make this organization explicit and/or tell something about the tempo.

be compared. It was necessary to have a considerable number of pieces
which could be dated with some accuracy, and since I was certain that mensural practice varied from composer to composer, it was necessary that
these pieces be by the same composer. Dufay was the obvious choice: his
life spanned three-quarters of the century; several hundreds of works attributed to him have been preserved; and many of these pieces can be dated.

        The nature of my investigation was such that most modern tran-
scriptions were useless. Each piece was studied in its original notation.
I grouped them according to notational characteristics and used datable
works in each group as a basis for suggesting limiting dates for the entire
group. Compositions which were written at about the same time should have
common features, which can just as well be details of notation as general
musical characteristics. I carried out this procedure in as inflexible a
way as possible, even when there was reason to suspect that certain works
did not belong where this method placed them. There may be mistakes in my
chronology. I do not believe they are numerous, and I thought it preferable not to make any concessions in my procedure on the basis of other
evidence.

        These groups of the Dufay works, nine of them arranged in what I
take to be the proper chronological order, form the skeleton of this book.
I should say immediately that there is nothing startling about a chronology
of all the works of this composer. So much sound research has been done in
the Dufay era in recent years, a major share of it by Heinrich Besseler,
that a chronology could be constructed on other types of evidence which
would agree substantially with mine. Compositions which scholars have always assumed were early works fall early in my chronology, those known to
be late fall in one of my later groups; pieces found only in early manuscripts turn up in one of my first groups, pieces found only in later
sources turn up late. But this is the first attempt at a comprehensive
chronology,[5] and I date pieces with more precision than would be possible
in a chronology based on manuscript studies or stylistic analyses of the
music.

        Besseler, in the seventh chapter of his _Bourdon und Fauxbourdon_[6]
and in a recent article,[7] has been a pioneer in the technique of using
signatures and mensurations to date certain works and groups of pieces. I
will take exception to some of his assertions and conclusions in the course

---

[5]   I have examined 224 compositions attributed to Dufay, in one or more of
their manuscript sources; these are listed in Appendix A, grouped by type
of composition. The manuscripts which were available to me in facsimile or
on microfilm are listed, with their abbreviations, in Appendix B; there
were 59 of these.

[6]   Heinrich Besseler, _Bourdon und Fauxbourdon_ (Leipzig, 1950).

[7]   H. Besseler, "Dufay in Rom," AfMW, 15 (1958), pp. 1-19.

of this book, but this is not meant to obscure the fact that his findings
are valid and useful, on the whole, and that he was the first to attempt
this method.

Around each group I have woven discussions of problems of notation and performance practice brought up by the pieces in the group, often
comparing Dufay's practices with those of other composers in an attempt to
show where Dufay's usages originated and which musicians seem to have been
influenced by them.

The most obvious fruit of my study is the chronology, but another
and perhaps equally important purpose of this book is to present a more
systematic picture of fifteenth-century notational practice than has been
given before. I will spend no more time than is necessary in pointing out
mistakes and confusions in other works on notation, but I must say at this
point that the one basic mistake in most of these has been the assumption
that the "rules" of notation remained constant throughout the fifteenth and
sixteenth centuries, that there was one notational practice during this
period, and that what was valid for Palestrina must have been valid for
Ockeghem and Dufay.

My study is based on the assumption that mensuration and signatures, as well as other details of notation, found in manuscripts of the
period are those intended by Dufay. It might seem possible that scribes
made so many alterations, intentional or otherwise, that it would be impossible to reconstruct Dufay's practice. In the course of my study I examined a total of 224 compositions ascribed or attributed to Dufay. Some of
these have come down to us in only one manuscript, and there is no way of
checking their mensurations and signatures. But where there were two
sources for a piece I was able to check between the two manuscripts; if
there were three sources, I could make two different checks; if a work was
found in four manuscripts, three checks were possible; and so on. In all,
I was able to compare the same piece between two manuscripts 367 times, but
even this figure does not give an accurate picture of the amount of checking I was able to do on this point. Dufay wrote for three, four, or five
voices, and in every piece the mensuration and signature of each of these
voices could be checked. In addition, many of the Dufay works have changes
of mensuration; an isorhythmic motet may have ten or more different signatures among all voices, and a complete mass might have three or four times
as many.

I did not find a single instance of disagreement as to mensuration.
The only disagreement between signatures are:

> Invidia *inimichi*, the final section, C in BU and Ox, but Ɔ
>   in FP;
> Supremum *est*, middle section, ₵ 3 in BL, Tr92, and BU, but C 3
>   in Mod B;

  Lauda syon, verse 14, O in Tr92 but Φ in Tr93;

  Nuper rosarum, tenor, O ¢ ¢ Φ in Tr92 but O C ¢ Φ in Mod B;

  Vexilla regis, superius, changes from Φ to O in Tr92 but
   remains in Φ throughout in ModB and RS15;

  Magnificat octavi toni, "Deposuit ..." verse, Φ in SPB80 but O
   in Tr92 and ModB;

  Magnificat quinti toni, "Sicut locutus ..." verse, Φ in ModB
   but O in FM112;

  Belle vueilles moy vengier, C in MC but ¢ in FM176;

  Vostre bruit, C in FM176 but ¢ in all other sources;

  Missa ave regina celorum, ¢ in all five sections in SPB80 but
   C in these places in Br5557 and ModE;

  Missa Caput, C in Tr89 but ¢ in Tr90 and Tr93.

With no disagreement at all on mensurations and with disagreement
on signatures no more than a small fraction of a per cent (and with only
one exception the differences being nothing more than the presence or absence of the stroke calling for diminutum which, as will be shown later, is
more a tempo indication than a change in mensuration), there is every reason
to assume that since scribes were remarkably accurate about such matters,
they have given us faithful copies of what Dufay himself wrote down.

  Appendix B is a list of manuscripts used in this study, with
their abbreviations. I have used the most widely accepted abbreviations,
giving preference to those used in publications of the American Institute
of Musicology. My only intentional deviation is in the use of "Ox" to
refer to the manuscript Oxford, Bodleian Library, Canonici misc. 213 rather
than the usual "O," to avoid confusion with the symbol for tempus perfectum.

  Appendix A is a list of all the Dufay works. Mass cycles come
first, followed by settings of individual sections of the ordinary, motets,
short liturgical pieces, and finally, secular works; the pieces in each
group are arranged alphabetically. I have given the number of the chronological group in which I placed each piece, and since I devote one chapter
to each of these groups, this number also refers to the chapter in which
the work is discussed. Following the title of each work in this appendix,
I have listed all manuscripts in which I have located it, with location by
page. This concordance is my own work and is undoubtedly incomplete in
some few details, since a handful of manuscripts which may contain some of
the Dufay works was not available to me. I have included it because I believe it to be substantially complete, and because no other comprehensive
concordance of the compositions of Dufay is available in print.

  There has been some misunderstanding as to what the word, "motet"
meant at this time. My classification of a piece as a motet or as a short
liturgical piece was done on the basis of type of setting, not the text.
A sequence text set as a simple three-part harmonization of the chant melody

is a short liturgical piece, a similar text made into a longer and more
elaborate piece is a motet. In this I have followed the practice of the
scribe of ModB who, in his index, after an extensive group of brief settings
of hymns, magnificats, and antiphons, prefaced a section of more complicated
pieces with the remark "hic incipiunt motteti."

There is an acute problem of pagination with certain of the manuscripts of this period, and I can best illustrate my solution by describing
the situation in one of the more troublesome sources, BL. The manuscript
itself has two different paginations: each piece, or section of a piece,
has a roman numeral on the verso of each opening, running from 1 to 339.
In addition — or more accurately, originally — each folio has a roman numeral in the upper right-hand corner of the recto of each opening. There are
difficulties with each of these systems. With the first, when a piece is
added at the bottom of a page or opening, it has no number; also, since a
new number is found on each opening, whether a new piece begins there or
the music is a continuation of the composition found on the previous opening, a work which takes up two openings will have two numbers, one which
takes up three will have three numbers. With the second system, some numbers were skipped (172-177, for example), and the three fascicles (11, 12
and 20) inserted in the manuscript after this pagination was put in do not
share in it, having their own system of page numbering.

De Van's inventory[8] assigns a number to each composition; by his
count there are 328 pieces. Besseler, Reaney, and other scholars have
adopted this numbering in their writings and inventories. When they refer
to BL 213, this does not mean folio 213 or the 213th composition according
to the numbering in the manuscript itself, but to the piece which de Van
has listed as 213 in his inventory.

My own choice in this matter was dictated by a strong prejudice
against any practice in a work of scholarship which puts an obstacle in the
path of someone else working in the same area. The use of de Van's numbering as the only reference to a piece forces the student or scholar working
with the manuscript itself to refer continually to the journal containing
the inventory in order to find out just what piece is under discussion and
where it is located in the manuscript. In this era of the microfilm reader,
it is hardly an exaggeration to say that almost anyone with enough interest
in the music of the fifteenth century to read a technical article or book
about it will have access to films of some or all of the manuscripts referred to, and I believe that references to pieces in these sources should
enable the reader to locate the proper spot in the manuscript with a mini-
mum of bother.

---

[8] G. de Van, "Inventory of Manuscript Bologna, Liceo Musicale, Q 15
(olim 37)," MD, 2 (1948), pp. 231-257.

Suppose a scholar working with the Grossim motet _Imera_ _dat_ _hodierno_
in Ox finds it necessary to compare this version with those in other manuscripts. Turning to the Reaney inventory,[9] he will find the following concordances listed: BL 203; BU 66; Em 156; PC f. 63[v]; Tr 1481. When he views
the film of the first of these, he will find that "BL 203" is of no help in
locating the piece until he fetches the de Van inventory and decodes this
inscription. Likewise, "BU 66" does him no good at all until he refers to
the Besseler inventory[10] of this manuscript; "Tr 1481" is meaningless without the proper volume of the DTO;[11] and "Em 156" needs to be translated into more useful form by the Dèzes inventory.[12] Thus he must refer to four
separate places in addition to the original inventory in order to find the
various copyings of this piece.

In my opinion, this is a cumbersome and bothersome system, and I
have rejected it in my work. Rather than the de Van numbering of BL, I
have used the original numbering (not foliation) of the manuscript itself.
There is no valid objection to this system, after all. If a work covers
three openings and therefore has three numbers, I cannot see that it is
confusing in any way to refer to it as, for example, BL 37-39. If there
are two pieces on one opening, it is clear enough to call the first BL 260
and the second BL 260[b]. I have used the foliation in Ox rather than the
numbering system of the Reaney inventory; I have used the numbering used in
BU, whereby each page rather than each recto is given a number, rather than
Besseler's numbering; I have referred to pieces in the Trent codices by
their foliation rather than the number assigned them in the thematic index;
pieces in Ao are identified by foliation, not by the numbering of the the de
Van inventory;[13] I have not used Besseler's numbering for any of the manuscripts inventoried by him in his monumental work on the sources of this
period.[14] As a result, any piece mentioned in this book can be located in
any manuscript in which it is found, quickly and without referring to anything else.

All references to masses, motets, short liturgical pieces and sec-

---

[9] Gilbert Reaney, "The Manuscript Oxford, Bodleian Library, Canonici Misc.
213," MD, _9_ (1955), pp. 73-104.

[10] H. Besseler, "The Manuscript Bologna Biblioteca Universitaria 2216,"
MD, _6_ (1952), pp. 39-65.

[11] G. Adler and O. Koller, "Sechs Trienter Codices. Erste Auswahl," DTO,
VII (Vienna, 1900).

[12] Karl Dèzes, "Der Mensuralcodex des Benediktinerklosters Sancti Emmerami
zu Regensburg," ZfMW, _10_ (1927), pp. 65-105.

[13] G. de Van, "A Recently Discovered Source of Early Fifteenth Century
Polyphonic Music," MD, _2_ (1948) pp. 5-74.

[14] H. Besseler, "Studien zur Musik des Mittelalters II," AfMW, _8_ (1927),
pp. 137-258.

ular works will be by title only. Settings of the same sections of the ordinary of the Mass are numerous and I will differentiate between them by
identifying each according to its location in one manuscript. To insure a
common denominator among as many pieces as possible, any mass section found
in BL will be designated by its number in this manuscript, no matter where
else it is found, since BL contains the largest number of these pieces. If
it is not in BL, I have given its location in one of the Trent codices.
Since with only one exception all mass sections attributed to Dufay are
found either in BL or one of the Trent manuscripts, this is a simple solution to what could have been made into a complicated matter. I have followed a similar method of identification with the several pairs of other
pieces with identical texts.

      Since I constantly refer to "breves," "semibreves," "flagged semi-
minims," and the like, I have retained original shapes of these notes in my
musical examples, which therefore belong to the category of unreduced transcriptions. I have put all voices in treble and bass clefs, though I have
indicated the original clef in each case, and for convenience I have drawn
bar lines, every minim, semibreve, or breve depending on the mensuration of
the particular piece and the points illustrated by the example. I have not
become involved in the controversial matters of text underlay and editorial
accidentals, but have simply reproduced what I found in the original sources.
I have retained the spelling of the period, in titles and texts.

ACKNOWLEDGEMENTS

This study, in its original form, was my doctoral dissertation at Princeton University. I am grateful to the Department of Music of the school for making publication of this revised version possible by sharing printing costs with the Princeton University Press.

Gwynn S. McPeek generously made his large personal collection of microfilms of fifteenth century manuscripts available to me when we were colleagues at Newcomb College, Tulane University. Gustave Reese made a large number of most valuable suggestions and also sent me films of manuscripts I had not seen. Dragan Plamenac kindly sent me a copy of his film of a Munich manuscript that had eluded me; Kenneth Levy made a careful reading of a Dufay work in a source unavailable to me at the time; Edward Lerner called my attention to several concordances I had missed. I acknowledge, with gratitude, the assistance of these scholars.

Oliver Strunk offered penetrating and useful suggestions after seeing this study in its first version; my indebtedness to him goes far beyond this, however.

Mrs. William Hanle of the Princeton Press was of invaluable assistance in the preparation of the manuscript for press. Her careful reading, followed by pointed questions and suggestions, resulted in a tightening of the text and format.

Professor Paul Brainard of Brandeis University, after a remarkably careful and close reading of the first printing of this book, sent me a list of mistakes and misprints which facilitated the preparation of a second printing.

CONTENTS

FIGURES AND TABLES

CONTENTS

Lists of the Dufay Works by Groups

A CHRONOLOGY OF THE WORKS OF GUILLAUME DUFAY

CHAPTER I

EARLIEST WORKS, <u>ca</u>. 1415-1423

The first trace of Dufay is at Cambrai, where he was an altar boy from 1409 to 1411. His first compositions must have been written there under the influence and guidance of Richard Loqueville, who had charge of the music at the cathedral from 1413 until his death in 1418. One can further assume that the music of both Loqueville the teacher and Dufay the student was influenced by compositions of the most famous musician of the day, Johannes Ciconia, who died in 1411. Since the manuscripts BL and Ox preserve pieces by Ciconia, Loqueville, and Dufay, the Ciconia works in these sources must be his later compositions, the ones still known and sung when Dufay was learning his trade from Loqueville. They are, with their mensurations:

BL 4-5	Et in terra	(₵) ₵ ₵O₵ ₵
BL 6-7	Patrem	(₵)
BL 92-93	Et in terra	(O)
BL 94-95	Patrem	(₵)
BL 97	Et in terra	(O)₵
BL 184	Et in terra	(O)
BL 185-186	Patrem	(₵)
BL 249	O felix templum	(O)
BL 274	Petrum Marcello	(O)
BL 281	O virum omnimoda	(O)
BL 282	O beata incendium	₵
BL 283	O Padua sidus	₵
BL 284	Venece mundi splendor	(O)
BL 285	O Petre Christi	(₵)
BL 286	Ut per te omnis	(O)
BL 296	Doctorum principem	₵ O ₵
BL 297	Albane misse celitus	(₵)
Ox 101,102	Et in terra	(₵)

Signatures are rarely given at the beginning of a piece, on the assumption that the singer should be able to determine the mensuration himself, but when the mensuration changes in the course of a piece, there is always a signature to signal this change. ₵, O, and ₵ are the only initial mensurations used; movement in each of these is primarily in semibreves and minims, with a sprinkling of breves and with longs found only at cadences. A count of the notes of the superius part of the Et in terra (BL 184) gives:[1]

	longs	breves	semibreves	minims	semiminims
(O)	6	13	113	157	---

Longs are invariably found in patterns which would have caused them to be imperfected, even if there had been a signature suggesting that they be perfect. In this piece, and in all of Ciconia's works, the singer needed to concern himself only with tempus and prolation; major and minor mode were matters for theorists, not performers. Ciconia's tenors sometimes move in semibreves and minims with the upper voice, sometimes in breves and semibreves. Semiminims appear in only 3 of the 18 pieces (BL 97, BL 284, BL 285), and in these only in ornamental fashion.

Besseler, in the seventh chapter of Bourdon und Fauxbourdon, suggests that around 1430 major prolation was abandoned in favor of tempus perfectum. He offers the following table in partial support of this contention:[2]

manuscript	no. of pieces	6/8	3/4	other
Ox 5-6 (ca. 1420/25)	59	47(= 80%)	5(= 8%)	7(= 12%)
Ox 4 (ca. 1430/35)	42	12(= 29%)	28(= 66%)	2(= 5%)
EscB (ca. 1435)	34	3(= 9%)	31(= 91%)	0(= 0%)

This looks convincing enough, but in the case of the fascicles from Ox, he is comparing dissimilar things. Fascicles 5 and 6 contain nothing but French rondeaux, virelais and ballades (with the exception of three Italian ballatas and one inserted motet); this is a limited repertoire, and the mensural practice cannot be assumed to be representative of all types of pieces written at this time. Fascicle 4 also contains French secular works, but there are, in addition, 14 mass sections and motets, comprising one-third of the contents of the fascicle.

The thesis that major prolation was little used after around 1430 is valid and useful, but it is by no means true that minor prolation was rarely used before 1430.[3] The 18 pieces by Ciconia listed above were written well before 1430, but only four are in major prolation throughout, and

---

[1]   The count in all such tables in this book will be of the superius voice only, unless otherwise specified.

[2]   Besseler, Bourdon und Fauxbourdon, p. 124. He transcribes ₵ as 6/8 and O as 3/4.

[3]   Rehm, in his edition of the Binchois chansons (Musikalische Denkmäler 2), offers a chronology of these works. With only one exception, the pieces which he dates before 1430 are in major prolation and those which he dates after this year are in minor.

only three others have sections in this mensuration. The use of major prolation in a composition from the first half of the fifteenth century suggests strongly that it was written before <u>ca</u>. 1430, but the use of minor
prolation is of no help in determining when it was written.

The few pieces by Loqueville which have come down to us resemble
the Ciconia works in their mensural usage:

BL 22	Sanctus	O
BL 61	Et in terra	₵ ₵ ₵ ₵ ₵
BL 78	Et in terra	(O)
BL 79	Patrem	(O)
BL 280	O flos in divo	(₵) O
Ao 80'82	Et in terra	₵ ₵ ₵
Ox 90	Quant compaignons	₵
Ox 91'92	Je vous pri	₵
Ox 93'	Qui ne veroit	₵
Ox 93'	Puis que je suy	₵
Ox 96'	Pour mesdisans	₵

Only ₵ , O , and C are used, and movement in all three mensurations is
in semibreves and minims.

Using these works of Ciconia and Loqueville as a model, I have
brought together as group 1 all Dufay works which: a) use C , O , and
₵ as initial mensurations: b) move mainly in semibreves and minims,
though the tenor may have breve-semibreve movement; and c) contains no semiminims. My assumption is that this group contains his very earliest works,
written while he was under the influence of the "northern" music of such
men as Ciconia and Loqueville, at Cambrai or soon after he came to Italy
for the first time, which was probably a few years before 1420. I have assigned the dates <u>ca</u>. 1415-1423 to this group—<u>ca</u>. 1415 because if Dufay was
born around the turn of the century, as seems likely, he could not have been
writing music much before this date, and 1423 because this is the date of
the latest datable piece in the group. Also, works datable soon after this
year are already different in certain important respects, as will be shown
later.

All pieces in the group which can be dated precisely or approximately do indeed fall within the period suggested. BL 21, the <u>Sanctus qui
ianuas mortis</u>, is a three-voice rewriting of the Loqueville[4] <u>Sanctus</u> which
follows it in the manuscript and must date from the period when Dufay was
Loqueville's student at Cambrai. Besseler groups the <u>Kyrie</u> (BL 17) and the

---

[4]   It has been assumed that the piece is by Loqueville; the actual inscription is "Vineus secundum Loqueville."

Agnus Dei (BL 23) with it to form a short mass;[5] these two sections must
have been written at about the same time as the Sanctus. Dufay scholars,
without exception, have taken the Missa sine nomine to be his earliest preserved complete setting of the ordinary,[6] dating from well before the Missa
Sancti Jacobi of the mid-1420's. The motet Vasilissa ergo was written in
celebration of the wedding of Cleophe de Malatesta to Theodore, despot of
Morea; de Van dates this marriage in 1421,[7] Besseler 1419-1420.[8] Resveilles
vous has to do with the marriage of Carlo Malatesta in 1423. All pieces in
the group are found in manuscripts containing the oldest repertoire, such
as BU, Ao, Tr92, Tr87, and the first part of BL. Furthermore, I know of no
Dufay piece which mensural usage places in another of my groups which is
suspected of being an early work.[9]

　　　The exclusion of all pieces with semiminims probably keeps out
some compositions which were written in the period 1415-1423. If Dufay did
follow the practice of Ciconia and Loqueville, a certain small percentage
of his works written at this time made use of a few semiminims. But I
thought it preferable to exclude a few pieces then make the limitations of
the group flexible enough to admit not only these pieces but also others
which do not belong here at all.

　　　Since basic movement is in semibreves and minims in each of the
three basic mensurations, it would seem that there would be no difference
in tempo among them. But the word "tempo" is meaningless in the preceding
statement unless it is understood to refer to the rate of speed of one type
of note; to say that the tempo remains constant between two mensurations
means one thing if it is assumed that the semibreve was the unit of measure
and something quite different if the minim is taken as this unit. In the
first case, a change from C to ₵ would take a third away from the duration of the minim, giving the effect—in modern terminology—of a change to
triplet rhythm and a feeling that motion has accelerated. If the minim remains constant, on the other hand, a change from C to ₵ gives the effect
of a change from 2/4 (or 2/8) to 3/4 (or 3/8), with quarters (or eighths)
remaining constant; this lengthening of the measure gives the effect of a
broadening of tempo.

---

[5]　H. Besseler, Guglielmi Dufay: Opera Omnia, IV, xiii.

[6]　Though I am not convinced that Dufay's original intention was to have
the five sections of this "mass" go together, cf. my article "Manuscript
Structure in the Dufay Era," Acta 34, 1962, pp. 180-181, in which I suggest
that this is a composite, not complete, mass.

[7]　G. de Van, Guglielmi Dufay: Opera Omnia, I, iii.

[8]　Besseler, Bourdon und Fauxbourdon, p. 73.

[9]　Though Besseler, in "Dufay in Rom," suggests that certain pieces in my
Group 1 were written while Dufay was in Rome as a member of the Papal Choir
between the years 1429 and 1433.

Musical Example 1: Dufay, Gloria of <u>Missa</u> <u>sine</u> <u>nomine</u> (Ao 32'33)

<u>Belle</u> <u>que</u> <u>vous</u>, a three-voice piece with one voice moving in each of the
three basic mensurations, works only if minim equivalence is assumed among
these mensurations.

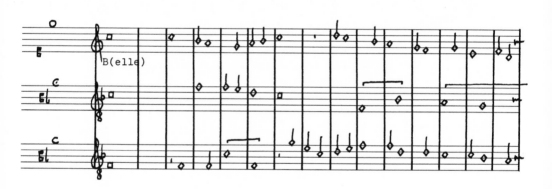

Musical Example 2: Dufay, <u>Belle</u> <u>que</u> <u>vous</u> (Tr87 136')

If minims are constant among them when they occur simultaneously, they must
be the normal unit of measure.

Coloration is used sparingly in pieces of Group 1, turning up
most commonly in C at the semibreve level: a colored semibreve loses a
third of its value, one minim, so that three colored semibreves, or their
equivalent, occupy the space normally taken up by two semibreves. If C
is transcribed in 6/8, this type of coloration has the effect of shifting
the rhythm to 3/4.

Musical Example 3: Dufay, Patrem (Tr92 118'119)

I will refer to this as semibreve level, where the normal 2 × 3 pattern is
replaced by a temporary 3 × 2. It is true that breves in such coloration
patterns also lose a third of their value, one semibreve, but there is no
suggestion of a shift to 3/2, with one 3/2 measure replacing two 6/8 measures, which would result if the composer had thought in terms of a rhythmic shift at the breve level.

          Minim coloration is also found in ₵ , with three colored minims
replacing two normal ones. In such a passage it is possible to find a colored semibreve which has the value of two colored minims. Such a semibreve
appears to have lost a third of its normal value, as in semibreve coloration, but it is simply a replacement for two colored minims, and the rhythmic shift is felt at the minim level.

          Flos florum, which is in tempus perfectum throughout, uses both
minim coloration and breve coloration, in which three colored breves, or
their equivalent, replace two normal breves. If O is transcribed as 3/4,
minim coloration can be shown as eighth-note triplets and breve coloration
by the replacement of two 3/4 bars by one 3/2 bar, the semibreve (or, in
transcription, the quarter note) remaining constant.

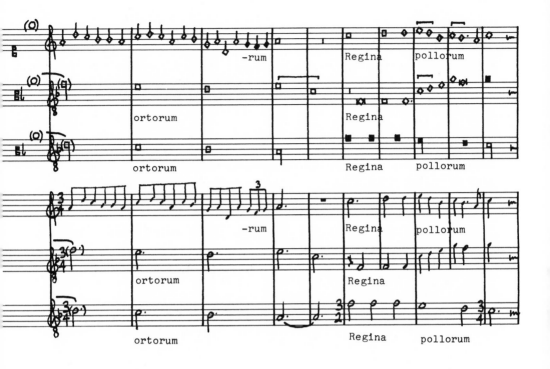

Musical Example 4: Dufay, _Flos_ _florum_ (Ox 25'26)

Coloration in C brings about a more complex situation in
Invidia _inimica_, in which semibreve coloration has the effect of replacing
two normal semibreves by three colored ones as in ₵ . But while the minim

Musical Example 5: Dufay, _Invidia_ _inimica_ (Ox 128'129)

remains constant between colored and noncolored sections in Ȼ, in this passage in C, three colored semibreves of two minims each replace two normal semibreves of two minims each. Three semibreves replace two, six minims replace four, the colored breve loses a third of its value—no note remains constant between the voice in coloration and the other two voices. If C were to be transcribed as 2/4, the section in coloration would have to be written as eighth-note triplets, or it would have to be put in 6/8, with a dotted quarter note equaling a quarter note of the basic meter.

In other Dufay works in C, only minim coloration is found; Invidia inimica is the only piece in this mensuration with semibreve coloration. It is found in BU and OX, attributed to Dufay in both sources, and also in FP, one of the important sources of fourteenth-century Italian music. It is an insertion in the latter manuscript, in white notation, and it is impossible to tell just when it was copied; but the fact that it is a three-voice piece in FP but has four voices in Ox and BU suggests that the FP version is nearest the original. It is anonymous in FP, a suspicious situation if this is indeed the earliest of the three sources. It is possible that the piece, in an original version for three voices, was written by some Italian composer and that Dufay merely added a fourth voice. It was not uncommon at this time for a musician to add a voice to a piece written by someone else; several instances in which Dufay himself did this will be mentioned in succeeding chapters. Originally, Dufay's name may have been placed next to the added voice and only later found its way to the top of the entire piece.

Ma belle dame je vous pri has a signature of ☉ in all three voice parts, with movement in semibreves and minims. Dufay employed this mensuration in the tenor of some of his more elaborate pieces, masses, and motets, but this is his unique usage of it as a mensuration in all voices of a piece. ☉ shows up most often, in the first third of the century, in flamboyant "polyrhythmic" pieces, but it is also found as an initial signature in a scattering of simpler works. Though Ma belle dame ... is the only piece attributed to Dufay which uses ☉ as a basic mensuration, his treatment of it is consistent with his general mensural practice; there is no other reason to question its authenticity, and I have placed it in Group 1 because it contains no semiminims.

In Resveillies vous, dating from 1423, Dufay uses the ciphers 2 and 3 in the course of sections in Ȼ and O. Neither Ciconia nor Loqueville made use of such ciphers; Dufay must have learned this practice from Italian or French composers after coming to Italy. It is necessary to proceed with caution in discussing "proportions," which have caused such confusion among theorists of the fifteenth and twentieth centuries, and I will merely explain the functions of these ciphers in this particular piece.

Transcription reveals that the cipher 3 in the course of the mensuration ○ causes three minims to replace two.

Musical Example 6: Dufay, Resveillies vous (Ox 126)

The remarkable thing here is the use of 3 to bring about a relationship which would seem to be more accurately designated by 3/2. ⊙ and (○)3 have a similar organization, with three semibreves per breve and three minims per semibreve, but there is a difference between the two. Assuming minim equivalence between mensurations in major prolation and those in minor, two minims of ○ would equal two minims of ⊙ . Since the function of the cipher 3 is to replace two minims by three, three minims of (○)3 equal two minims of ⊙ . The two mensurations, similar in organization, go at different tempi.

(O)2 appears briefly, long enough to make it clear that twenty-four minims of this mensuration replace six semibreves, or twelve minims, of O (See Musical Example 6). The cipher 2 seems to announce that two minims are to replace each minim of the original mensuration. Since four minims of (O)2 replace two of O, and two minims of O make up one semibreve, two semibreves of two minims each (or one breve) of (O)2 equal one semibreve of two minims of O. The function of the cipher 2 can be explained in several ways, then: it replaces one minim by two; is signals a duple proportion, with a breve replacing the semibreve of the original; or it shifts the organization of the basic mensuration one place to the left.

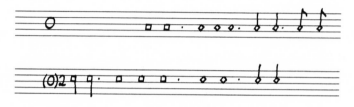

Musical Example 7: organization of O and (O)2.

The use of 2 in the course of a section in ℂ brings about a similar situation. Six minims of (ℂ)2 replace three of ℂ , setting up what might be described as a duple proportion, with a semibreve of (ℂ)2 replacing a minim of ℂ . There are three semibreves to the breve and two minims to the semibreve under (ℂ)2, which is the organization of ℂ shifted one place to the left.

Musical Example 8: Dufay, <u>Resveillies</u> <u>vous</u> (Ox 126')

Once again we see two different signatures, O and (ℂ)2, resulting in

mensurations with the same organization, but once again there is a difference between them. Assuming minim equivalence between O and C, two
minims (or one semibreve) of O equal two minims of C. Since a minim of
C equals a semibreve of (C)2, two minims of C equal two semibreves of
(C)2, which equal two minims (or one semibreve) of O. Thus one semibreve
(of two minims) of O equals two semibreves (each of two minims) of (C)2,
and the two are in duple proportion.

     The cipher 3 occurring in the course of the mensuration (C)2
causes two minims of the first mensuration to be replaced by three, giving
an organization of three semibreves to the breve and three minims to the
semibreve, the same organization found under ⊙ and (O)3. But again there
is no duplication. It was shown above that two minims of ⊙ equal three
minims of (O)3. Assuming minim equivalence between O and C, two minims
of O(or three minims of O3) equal two minims of C — or two semibreves of
two minims each of C2, or two semibreves of three minims each of (C2)3.
Thus two minims of ⊙ equal three minims of (O)3 or six minims of (C2)3.

     To summarize, Dufay's earliest compositions make almost exclusive
use of the three mensurations C, O, and C, and of the simplest patterns
of coloration under these. Movement in all mensurations is in semibreves
and minims, and there are no semiminims. The ciphers 2 and 3 appear at the
very end of this first period. There is no trace of such signatures as
¢ and φ.

THE WORKS OF GROUP 1
(ca. 1415-1423)

Distinguishing characteristics: use of ₵ , C and O as basic
mensurations; semibreve-minim movement in each; no semiminims.

Missa sine nomine
    Kyrie   (₵)O
    Et in terra   (₵)₵O
    Patrem   (C)
    Sanctus   (₵)OC
    Agnus Dei   (₵)O

Kyrie BL 187 - Et in terra BL 187[b] - Patrem BL 188
  (O)   (C)   (C)

Kyrie BL 17 - Sanctus BL 21 - Agnus Dei BL 23
  (O)   (O)   (O)

Et in terra BL 40[10] - Patrem BL 41-42
  (C)   (C)

Et in terra BL 35-36 - Patrem BL 37-39
  (₵)O   (₵)O

Et in terra Tr92 120'121
    ₵O₵

Et in terra (ad modum tube) BL 180   Flos florum
    (C)   (O)

Ave virgo que de celis   Vasilissa ergo gaude
    (O)   (O)

---

[10] Attributed to Dufay in Ox but to Hugo de Lantins in Ao and BL.

Letabundus exsultet Tr92 68'69
C O C C O

Belle que vous
O / C / C

Ce jour de l'an
C

Entre vous
C

Helas et quant vous
(O)

Invidia inimica
(C) C

J'ay mis con cuer
(C)

Je donne a tous
(O)

Je requier a tous
(O)

Je veul chanter
(C)

L'alta belleza
(C)

Ma belle dame je vous pri
☉

Mon cuer me fait
(O)

Navre je suy
(O)

Par droit je puis complaindre
(C)

Passato e il tempo
superius: O 3 O 3 O
T, CT: O

Pour ce que veoir
(C)

Resveillies vous
superius: (C)2 C O 2 O 3 C 2 3 C
T, CT: (C)   O   C
Resvelons nous
(O)

Se ma damme
(O)

CHAPTER 2

1423-1429

A closer look at the contents of the fifth and sixth fascicles of Ox, used by Besseler to illustrate the prevalence of major prolation before 1430, reveals something else of significance: of the 47 pieces in major prolation, 42 contain semiminims and only 5 do not; but not 1 of the 12 pieces in minor prolation has semiminims. This is a clue to the more important fact that while semibreve-minim movement prevails in major prolation, there is a detectable shift to the use of larger notes in pieces in minor prolation. For example:

	longs	breves	semibreves	minims	semiminims
Ox 82, Binchois					
Amoureux suy (C)	3	15	91	156	31
Ox 85, Vide					
Amans doubles (C)	1	4	33	64	10
Ox 89, Lebertoul					
Ma doulce amour (O)	13	48	61	45	-
Ox 96'97, Gran Guielmo					
Ma chiere (C)	2	-	50	6	-

This pattern can be found in many other pieces in the sources of this period. BL contains twelve settings of sections of the ordinary attributed to Zacharia, who was in the Papal Choir before Dufay, leaving in 1424 or 1425;[1] nine of these are in minor prolation and there is not a single semiminim in the lot, the other three are in C and each has semiminims. A count of the superius and contra voices of two of these reveals the same shift noted above:

	longs	breves	semibreves	minims	semiminims
BL 73, Et in terra (C)	1	43	133	226	28
BL 68, Et in terra (O)	38	150	203	58	-

---

[1] Fr. X. Haberl, "Die römische 'schola cantorum' und die Päpstlichen Kapellsänger bis zur Mitte des 16. Jahrhunderts," VfMW, 3 (1887), p. 220.

My explanation of this phenomenon will involve a discussion of time-beating, but this discussion must be put off until a troublesome term, "tactus," has been disposed of. Present-day scholars of mensural practice agree almost unanimously that an understanding of tempo and time-beating in the fifteenth century must be based on the tactus and certain connotations which the term carries with it. We read: "The whole system of mensural notation rests upon the principle of a fixed, i.e., unchangeable unit of time, the tactus, a beat in moderately slow speed (M.M. 50-60) which pervades the music of this period like a uniform pulse. The tactus is normally represented by the S:S=T, with the other notes being multiples or fractions thereof."[2] Auda states that "the tactus stands as nothing less than the fundamental element, the principal generator of the transcription and performance of polyphonic mensural music from its origin, i.e., from the thirteenth century, up until at least the middle of the seventeenth century."[3]

Apel and Auda are by no means alone in insisting that the concept of the tactus governs transcription and performance of music from a period which includes the Dufay era. De Van, in the preface to the first volume of the Dufay Opera Omnia, states that only his conviction that music of this time should be printed in a way which will make its structure visually apparent "prevents me from adopting the method of transcription elaborated by Dr. Tirabassi, which is, however, based upon a correct conception of the tactus doctrine."[4] Bukofzer speaks of the "regular flow of the tactus" in his introduction to the works of Dunstable.[5] Schünemann,[6] Praetorius,[7] and Sachs[8] likewise base their discussions of mensurations and tempo on the concept of a tactus, and even though they are concerned mostly with theorists and music of the sixteenth century, they insist that their conclusions are valid for the Dufay era as well.

---

[2] W. Apel, The Notation of Polyphonic Music, pp. 146-147.

[3] A. Auda, "Le tactus principe générateur de l'interprétation de la musique polyphonique classique," Scriptorium, 4 (1950), p. 44 ("Le tactus n'en demeure pas moins l'élément fondamental, le principe générateur de la transcription et de l'exécution de la musique mesurée et polyphonique depuis ses origines, c'est-à-dire depuis le XIIIe siècle jusqu'au milieu du XVIIe au moins.")

[4] G. de Van, Opera Omnia, I(1), p. v.

[5] Manfred Bukofzer (ed.), John Dunstable: Complete Works (London, 1953), p. xviii.

[6] Georg Schünemann, "Zur Frage des Taktschlagens und der Textbehandlung in der Mensuralmusik," SIMG, 10 (1908), pp. 73-114.

[7] Ernst Praetorius, "Die Mensuraltheorie des Franchinus Gafurius und der folgenden Zeit" (Leipzig, 1905).

[8] Curt Sachs, Rhythm and Tempo (New York, 1953).

But the term is never used by theorists writing during Dufay's lifetime. It does not appear in the writings of Tinctoris,[9] Ramos[10] (the first to discuss time-beating), Prosdocimus de Beldemandis,[11] or Guilielmus Monachus.[12] Adam de Fulda makes the first use of the term that I have been able to find, in his De musica of ca. 1490.

Most theorists of the sixteenth century do use the term tactus, explaining it as a regular beat and insisting that a certain number of breves, semibreves, minims, and semiminims are to be sung to one or more of these beats in each mensuration. Such discussions are often illustrated by tact tables in which the number of notes of each sort to be sung to one tactus in each mensuration is laid out graphically. Figure I is such a table, taken from the Micrologus of Ornithoparcus, 1517; similar tables are

FIGURE I
A RULE FOR TACT

A Semibreefe is all Signes (excepting the Signes of Diminution, Augmentation, and Proportions) is measured by a whole Tact, as in the example following appeareth:

⊙3	27	9	3	1		TO ONE STROKE	TO ONE STROKE	TO ONE STROKE
O3	27	9	3	1	✝			
C3	12	6	3	1	✝			
⊙2	12	6	2	1				
⊙	12	6	3	1				
C˙	8	4	2	1				
O	12	6	3	1	✝			
C	8	4	2	1	✝			
	⊓	⊓	□	◇	◇	♩ 4	♪ 8	♬ 16

The Table of Tact Resolved.
From Ornithoparcus, Micrologus (1517), as translated by Dowland in 1609.

---

[9] Johannes Tinctoris: Diffinitorium musicae (ca. 1474); Tractatus de notis et pausis; Tractatus de regulari valore notarum; Proportionale musices (ca. 1476).

[10] Bartolome Ramos, Musica practica, 1482.

[11] Prosdocimus de Beldemanis, Tractatus de contrapuncto, 1412.

[12] Guilielmus Monachus, De praeceptis artis musicae, ca. 1480.

given by Listenius, [13] Finck, [14] Schnegass, [15] and even Morley in his A Plaine
and Easy Introduction to Practicall Musicke of 1597. Such tables look impressively complete and authoritative—but they have more to do with theoretical speculation than with musical practice. At least half the signatures listed were obsolete by the time such tables began to appear, including all those with major prolation, which on rare occasion might turn up as
artificial signatures in the tenor of a cantus firmus mass but were otherwise almost completely unknown outside of theoretical treatises. Also
suspicious is the care with which each of the four levels—major mode,
minor mode, tempus, and prolation—are specified for each mensuration.
Breves were used sparingly in most mensurations found in music contempor-
aneous with these tables, and longs and maxims were encountered only at
cadences. Since prolation was always minor by this time, the only relationships of concern to the performing musician were tempus and sometimes minor
mode. And when we find completely different tact-tables in treatises by
other men, such as Tinctoris and Lanfranco, [16] containing signatures of C22,
O 33, and the like, which never show up in actual music (but are solemnly
listed and commented on by such recent writers as Sachs), it seems even
more evident that such tables were nothing more than theoretical erections
functioning primarily as a basis for theorizing argumentation.

      Attempts to reconcile the differences between these tables and
their accompanying discussions of mensural usage can only lead to further
confusion. Take, for example, the detail of just how fast the tactus should
go and which note should be given one tactus.

      Schünemann says, "As we have seen, the breve served, in part,
as the unit of measure in the fourteenth and fifteenth centuries." [17] He
offers a transcription of a piece by Dunstable, with arrows drawn to indicate that a breve or its equivalent is to be sung to one up and down beat,
then fixes the speed of this beat by saying, "the duration of one Takt, i.e.,
a single down-and-up beat, was accurately fixed. ...If we take 72 as the
average number of beats of the pulse per minute, this will give us the
speed (of the Takt)." [18]

---

[13] Nicolaus Listenius, Musica Nicolai Listenii, 1549.

[14] Hermann Finck, Practica musica, 1556.

[15] C. Schneegass, Isagoges musicae, 1596.

[16] Giovanni Maria Lanfranco, Scintilla di musica, 1533.

[17] G. Schünemann, op. cit., p. 84. ("Im 14. und 15. Jahrhundert noch zum
Teil galt, wie wir gesehen haben, die Brevis als Masseinheit.")

[18] Ibid. p. 88. ("Die Dauer eines Taktes, d.h. des einmaligen Nieder—und
Auf-schlagens, war genau festgelegt. ... Nehmen wir 72 Pulsschläge in der
Minute als Durchschnitt, so hätten wir die Dauer,")

- Apel suggests a speed of M.M. 50-60 for the tactus, after explaining that this tactus was on the semibreve during the period 1300-1450 and on the minim in the period of "white mensural notation."[19]

- Sachs tells us that "the tactus had two beats in opposite direction, each one measuring between M.M. 60 and 80. ...The normal, standard tactus, often called major or integer, represented the two beats by minims and hence comprised a semibreve."[20]

- Bukofzer, on page xviii of his preface to the Dunstable works, says that in general a tempo of quarter note ≅ 80-100 will be appropriate for this music. In his transcription a quarter note usually represents a semibreve of the original notation.

- Tirabassi has nothing to say about the speed of the tactus, but his disciple Auda explains that one tactus is comprised of two motions of the hand, that it generally falls on the semibreve, and the "this double motion corresponds to the duration of one beat of the pulse, thus being about 75-80 tactus per minute."[21]

Applying each of these interpretations to a piece in tempus perfectum from the Dufay period, say one of the hymn settings dating from shortly after 1430, we get:

Schünemann	semibreve = M.M.	216
Apel	semibreve = M.M.	50-60
	or	
	semibreve = M.M.	17-20
Sachs	semibreve = M.M.	30-40
Bukofzer	semibreve = M.M.	80-100
Tirabassi-Auda	semibreve = M.M.	75-80

The difficulty is that each of these men has attempted to apply theories of one period—which are not consistent even within this period—to another period. It would be better to forget the word "tactus" in a discussion of signatures, mensurations, and tempi of the Dufay period. There is no evidence that the term was known or used then, or that the connotations which it carried in the following century had anything to do with this earlier music.

---

[19] Apel, op. cit., p. 97.

[20] Curt Sachs, Rhythm and Tempo, p. 219.

[21] A. Auda, "Le Tactus clef de la paléographie musicale des XVe et XVIe siècles," Scriptorium, 2 (1948), p. 261. ("Ce double geste correspond a la durée d'un battement du pouls, soit un total d'environ 75-80 tactus par minute.")

    This is not to deny that some sort of time-beating was practiced
in the fifteenth century. Many works of visual art from the Dufay era show
one member of a group of performing musicians doing something with a hand,
or some fingers, which can be nothing but time-beating. Schünemann calls
attention to some of these paintings,[22] several of which are reproduced in
the Besseler article on "Chorbuch" in Die Musik in Geschichte und Gegenwart
and in the same author's Musik des Mittelalters und der Renaissance.[23] And
the practice of having some sort of visual or audible beat to keep performers together is a thoroughly natural, instinctive one which certainly was
in use well before the fifteenth century.

    But I have abandoned the term tactus in this book because it has,
today, the connotation of a quite special type of time-beating which: had
a steady, invariable rate of speed in all mensurations; normally fell on
the semibreve; and consisted of two distince motions, up and down. I can
find no evidence which suggests that any one of these three concepts is
valid for the first three-quarters of the fifteenth century, and I have attempted to find out about the time-beating situation of this period by
studying the music itself and by consulting only those theorists close to
this music or those who make specific mention of performance practice of
this time.

    The later tact tables agree in assigning the beat in C and in
⊙ to the semibreve, but there are many suggestions of another possibility
if one reads closely: that the beat in mensurations in major prolation was
on the minim. For example:

    - Ramos, in the second chapter of Book Three of his Musica
Practica of 1482, says, "...wherefore at the present time almost everyone
maintains, and will write it thus in their compositions, that the beat of
the measure under the signatures C and ⊙ is normally on the minim."[24]

    - Hermann Finck, in the section of Practica Musica of 1556 dealing
with prolation, says, "Perfect prolation is that in which semibreves are
made up of three minims, or the semibreve forms the normal tactus, but it
is measured, according to the practice cf ancient musicians, so that each
minim is given one common weedcutter's beat."[25]

---

[22] Schunemann, op. cit., pp. 75-76

[23] Potsdam, 1931.

[24] "...quod iam pro maiori parte omnes tenent et scribunt in compositione
pro hoc signo ⊙ vel hoc C , quod mensurae morula in minima teneatur
integra."

[25] "Perfecta prolatio est, ubi semibrevis tres minimas continet, aut semibrevis integro tactu, iuxta veterum Musicorum consuetudinem mensuratur, so
wirt eine minima einem gemeinem Krauthackerischen schlag gelten."

- Adam de Fulda, writing about 1490, defined the tactus and explained where it was to fall in each mensuration: "Tactus is a continuous motion with the purpose of holding the measure together. In the three mensurations ⊙2, ⊙ and ₵ the tactus is made on the minim."[26]

- Aron, commenting in his Toscanello of 1523 on Ramos' discussion of major prolation, says, "If the answer is given that Josquin and Obrecht always placed the measure on the minim in the signatures ⊙ and ₵, I believe that such a thing was done more from practice than by any rule. I learn that their predecessors, masters such as Busnois, Ockeghem and Dufay, and many others of this sort who were famous men in their day and in whom they put great faith, and whom they followed in this matter, put the measure on the minim; and this is not to be reproached, for Bartholomeo Ramos said that this practice of putting the measure on the minim in signatures with (prolation) dots was always observed, as I have said, by Ockeghem, Busnois and Dufay, and by Giovanni de Monte the teacher, and also by other famous men of this sort."[27]

A beat on the semibreve in ₵ and ⊙ results in three (colored) semibreves being sung against every two beats in the common semibreve coloration patterns in these mensurations. This is by no means impossible, but it would be much easier and lead to more accurate rhythms if the beat were on the minim, which remains constant between normal patterns and those in coloration. A perfect semibreve would get three beats, a colored semibreve, two.

Complex "polyrhythmic" pieces by such men as Baude Cordier, which use a number of different mensurations but are basically in major prolation, turn out to be much simpler to transcribe and perform if the beat is assumed to fall on the minim throughout. Example 9 is a transcription of the Cordier Amans ames, with bar lines marking off each minim of the basic mensurations O, ₵ and ⊙. Apel prints a facsimile of this piece, a transcription, a table purporting to clarify the significance of the various

---

[26] M. Gerbert (ed.), Scriptores ecclesiastici de musica, III (1784), p. 362. ("Tactus est continua motio in mensura contenta rationis. ⊙2. ⊙. ₵. In his tribus tactum facit minima.")

[27] "Si responde che se da Josquino, et da Obreth e stato usitato ponere la misura ne la minima in questi segni ⊙ ₵ credo che da loro tale cose sia piu presto stata fatta per autorita, che per ragione alcuna. Impero che gli loro predecessori et maestri come Busnois, Ocheghen, et Duffai, et altri assai a gli quali per essere a gli tempi loro stati huomini famosi, hanno prestato grande fede: et per tanto hanno seguitato tal modo, il quale modo cioe dare la misura ne la minima, non e da vituperare perche Bartholomeo Rami dice, che tal modo di dare la misura ne la minima de gli segni puntati: e stato (come ho detto) osservato da Ocheghen, Busnois et Duffai et da Giovanni di monte suo precetore: et anchora de altri huomini in questa facolta famosissimi."

Musical Example 9:   Cordier, <u>Amans ames</u> (Ox 123)

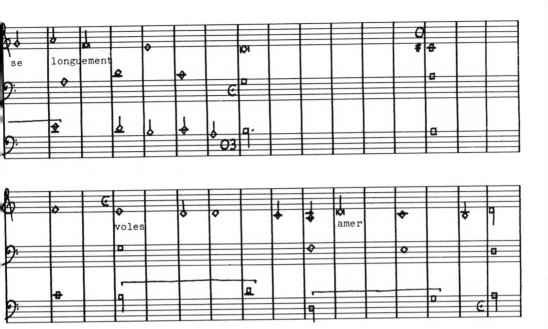

Musical Example 9: Cordier, Amans ames (Ox 123) completed

signatures, and the comment that the exact meaning of the latter must be
determined by experimentation.[28] The latter statement is misleading. In
this piece, as in all works of Cordier, there is minim equivalence among
O , C , C and ⊙ ; the cipher 2 or a line drawn through a signature
signals that two minims are to replace one; the cipher 3 calls for three
minims to replace one.

Transcription is simple once this consistent system is understood,
and apparent difficulties of performance likewise disappear with the assumption that there is minim equivalence throughout the piece with the beat on
the minim. Usual transcriptions of such pieces emphasize their "polyrhyth-
mis" nature.[29] Faced with such a transcription, the modern musician may
wonder how the piece was performed, or even question that it was performed
at all. But a musician of the early fifteenth century would have no difficulty; anchoring himself to the common denominator of the minim, he would
sing one minim or its equivalent to each beat in the basic mensurations or
two or three minims to each beat if so directed by a cipher or a line drawn

---

[28] Apel, op. cit., p. 175.

[29] For a transcription of this sort see Gilbert Reaney (ed.), Early Fifteenth Century Music, I, American Institute of Musicology, 1955, p. 7.

through a signature. Polyrhythmic structures at higher levels of mensuration would be left to take care of themselves.

      Thus there are hints both in the writings of theorists and in the
music itself that the beat was on the minim in pieces in major prolation
dating from the first part of the century.

      It was not until the end of the fifteenth century that theorists
first discussed the rate of speed of the beat. At first, they related it
to the human pulse. Compositions in major prolation from the early Dufay
era move in semibreves and minims, with a sprinkling of semiminims. A beat
on the minim at the rate of speed of the human pulse gives a tempo for these
pieces which is much too slow for my taste. But there is no necessity to
assume that the beat at this time, in major prolation, went at the same
speed as it did a half-century later, in other mensurations. I suggest that
it went quite a bit faster than the normal tactus of the sixteenth century—
Besseler suggests a tempo of minim = 150 for the Tapissier _Eya dulcis,_
in major prolation, which dates from the early years of the century[30]—and
Finck's remark about the "common weedcutter's beat" which he says was for-
merly used for pieces in major prolation can be taken to support this contention.

      It is probably futile to attempt to discover exactly how fast
this beat was. There were no mechanical means of setting a precise tempo in
the early fifteenth century, nor is there any reason to believe that an absolute measurement would have been desirable. Relating the speed of the
beat to the human pulse is appropriate. The latter varies from individual
to individual, and such factors as emotional state, age, climate, and weath-
er may cause variation in the same individual. The speed of the beat must
have varied according to whoever was entrusted with setting this beat, and
various factors could cause the same individual to vary his tempo from one
time to another. I believe that the beat on the minim in major prolation
was a fast beat, but I prefer not to guess just how fast it was. If one
were to assemble a group of musicians today and play for them a piece moving
in quarter notes at a tempo of M.M. 70, then at a tempo of M.M. 140, there
would be unanimous agreement that the latter tempo was "fast"; but if a
similar piece were to be given to each of them in turn with the request
that it be played at a "fast tempo, there would be considerable disagreement
on tempo. Things would have been no different in the fifteenth century.

      Turning now to mensurations in minor prolation, all tact-tables
agree that the beat was on the semibreve in O and   C , and nothing in the
music of the Dufay era or in what theorists have to say about this music
arouses suspicion that this is at variance with musical practice. The

---

[30] H. Besseler, "Studien zur Musik des Mittelalters II," AfMW, _8_ (1927),
pp. 213-214.

common breve coloration in O causes no difficulty, since the semibreve
remains constant between normal and colored passages, nor are there performance problems with minim coloration, with three minims or their equivalent
falling under a single beat. There is such unanimous agreement on this
point that I will not belabor the issue by quoting individual theorists.

I suggest, then, that in the first decades of the fifteenth century the normal practice was to have a fast beat on the minim in C —and
in the rare piece in ⊙ —but that in O and C the beat was on the semibreve. If there was minim equivalence between O and C , the beat on the
semibreve in O would be twice as slow as the fast beat on the minim in C ,
and there is no reason to believe that this was not the case in the Dufay
works of Group 1 and in the Ciconia and Loqueville pieces discussed in connection with these. But in the pieces mentioned at the beginning of this
chapter in which there is a shift of values between C and O , with semibreve-minim movement prevailing in the former and breve-semibreve movement
in the latter, there seems to be another tradition, one in which the beat
on the minim in C and that on the semibreve in O are not in a 2:1 ratio
but approach one another in speed, enough to necessitate some adjustment in
the note values used in the two mensurations. This adjustment is so extreme
in some pieces that the percentage of semibreves and minims in C approaches
the percentage of breves and semibreves, not semibreves and minims, in O ,
suggesting that minim equivalence between major and minor prolation was
giving way to a practice in which a minim in C was equated to a semibreve
in O .

In syllabic sections in C , Dufay generally changes syllables
every minim, another evidence that the minim was thought of as being the
basic unit in this mensuration. This is true of the works in my Group 1
and of those with which this chapter is concerned. But there is a percepti-
ble change of practice in minor prolation: in his earliest pieces, syllable
changes normally occur on the minim in O and C , just as in major prolation, but in those works in which there is a shift to movement in larger
notes in minor prolation, syllabic sections generally proceed with the semibreve as the smallest note on which the text changes.[31]

Since the shift to breve-semibreve movement in minor prolation is
not present in the works of such composers as Ciconia and Loqueville, or in
what I take to be the earliest works of Dufay, but is present in pieces
probably written in the first several decades of the century by Italian and
French composers, it seems likely that Dufay encountered this practice after
he had come to Italy.

---

[31] Cf. Robert Marshall, "The Mensural Practice of Gilles Binchois,"
Princeton (unpublished seminar report), 1961.

I have brought together as Group 2 all compositions by Dufay with sections in both major and minor prolation in which major prolation moves in semibreves and minims, with some semiminims, and minor prolation tends toward movement in breves and semibreves, with no semiminims. I suggest that these works were written between 1423 and 1429—the first date because pieces datable in 1421 and 1423 do not exhibit this tendency, the second because it would be exceptional for Dufay to use major prolation in a voice other than the tenor after this date. Only one piece in the group can be dated with any accuracy, the motet _Apostolo glorioso_ which Besseler says was written in 1426.[32]

There is another way of confirming that the pieces in this group were written no later than the third decade of the century. Two forms of the semiminim are found in manuscripts of the early Dufay period, one a minim with a flag added to the stem, the other a colored minim (i.e., a black minim in white notation or a white or red minim in black notation). Without going into the history of the two types at this point, I will point out here that they furnish a convenient means of separating the Dufay works into two groups falling on either side of the years 1431-1433; flagged semiminims are found in works written before this time, colored ones in those written afterwards. It might be questioned whether scribes were accurate enough about such a detail to enable us to use it as a tool, yet as was the case with signatures and mensurations, a check shows that scribes were remarkably accurate on this point. In the course of this study I was able to check a Dufay piece containing semiminims between two manuscripts 291 times, and in 285 of these instances there was agreement as to type of semiminim. The only exceptions were:

> Patrem BL 140-142
>   flagged semiminims in BL, Ao, Tr87, Tr92, colored in
>   Tr90, Tr93
>
> Kyrie BL 157
>   flagged semiminims in BL, colored in BU, Ao, Tr92
>
> Kyrie Tr87 94
>   flagged semiminims in Tr92, colored in Ao, Tr90, Tr93
>
> Supremum est
>   flagged semiminims in BU, colored in BL, ModB, Tr92
>
> O beate Sebastiane
>   flagged semiminims in BL, colored in ModB

---

[32] Besseler, _Bourdon und Fauxbourdon_, p. 73.

Several of these disagreements are not serious, involving as they
do Tr90 (and Tr93, which was copied from it), a notoriously inaccurate manuscript which will be discussed in a later chapter.

Every Dufay piece which we know to date from before 1431 has
flagged semiminims in every manuscript in which it is preserved, every Dufay piece which we know was written after 1433 has colored semiminims in
every manuscript. There is some overlap for the period 1431-1433: Supremum
est, dating from 1433, has flagged semiminims in one manuscript, as does the
ballade C'est bien raison which Besseler dates from the same year; while the
motet Ecclesie militantis, dated in 1431 by both de Van and Besseler, uses
colored semiminims in the only manuscript in which it is preserved, Tr87.[33]

Whether the change in semiminim type originated with Dufay or with
scribes of the day is not important—a piece by Dufay using flagged semiminims most probably was written no later than 1433, a piece using colored
semiminims most probably dates no earlier than 1431. Every composition in
my Group 2 uses the flagged form of the semiminim.

To recapitulate, Group 2 contains pieces with sections in both
major and minor prolation, with semibreve-minim movement and some flagged
semiminims in major and breve-semibreve movement with no semiminims in minor.
But Dufay certainly wrote other compositions during this period which are in
a single mensuration throughout and therefore cannot be put in this group.
I have brought together as groups 2^a and 2^b those pieces which satisfy the
requirements for one or the other of the basic mensurations of Group 2.

Group 2^a is made up of those pieces in major prolation throughout
which move in semibreves and minims and contain flagged semiminims. Most of
these works must date from 1423-1429, but since the only notational difference between these works and those of Group 1 is the absence of semiminims
in the latter, and since I pointed out in the previous chapter that in all
likelihood a few of Dufay's earliest works in ¢ contained a sprinkling of
semiminims, Group 2^a may contain some pieces dating from a slightly earlier
period. The methods used in this study cannot single out these works; so I
suggest dates of ca. 1415-1429 for Group 2^a. The two datable pieces fall in
this period: Adieu ce bons vins is dated 1426 in Ox, and the same manuscript tells us that Quel fronte signorille was written in Rome, where Dufay
joined the Papal Choir in 1428.

I have put in Group 2^b those works which satisfy the other half-
requirement for Group 2: they are in minor prolation throughout; there is a
shift to breve-semibreve movement; and there are no semiminims. I have also
included a handful of pieces in minor prolation with breve-semibreve movement

---

[33] But there is some question as to the accuracy of the date 1431 for this
work, as will be brought out later.

in which a scattering of flagged semiminims is found in ornamental patterns.
These pieces must date from after 1423 because of the shift towards movement in larger notes, and they must have been written before 1433, since no
Dufay piece datable after this year is void of semiminims or uses flagged
semiminims. Two of the works in this group are Je me complains, dated
"1425 adi. 12 lujo" in Ox, and Belle plaissant which is found in the sixth
fascicle of Ox and therefore must date from before 1426.

         As an illustration of the shift of values between major and minor
prolation in pieces from this period, I offer a count of Et in terra (BL
192) from Group 2, then of J'atendray tant from Group 2^a, and of Bon jour
bon mois from Group 2^b. The count is of the upper two voices in each case.

	longs	breves	semibreves	minims	semiminims
Et in terra (₵)	2	9	57	92	6
O	10	33	70	43	–
J'atendray (₵)	2	–	27	74	15
Bon jour (O)	3	43	109	39	6

         There are no instances of major prolation in one voice of a com-
position against minor prolation in another in the pieces which make up
these three groups, though this did occur in Belle que vous of Group 1. I
have avoided suggesting a rate of speed for the beat in Group 2, aside from
saying that the beat in ₵ was fast and that in O and C more moderate.
The fact that Dufay never used major and minor prolation simultaneously at
this period may be another evidence of the absence of any precise ratio between the rate of speed of the two and of the replacement of the minim
equivalence of his earlier works by a different relationship.

         Coloration is used more frequently than in the earlier works.
Semibreve coloration shows up in almost every piece in ₵ , breve coloration is common in O , and minim coloration is used in each of the basic
mensurations.

         The cipher 2 is used in O gemma lux and in Mon chier amy in the
same way as in several pieces in ₵ in Group 1, to signal an organization
of three semibreves per breve and two minims per semibreve, with a semibreve
of (₵)2 equivalent to a minim of ₵ . Mon chier amy uses the signature
(O)3 to show that three minims replace two, just as in Resveillies vous
of my first group, giving an organization of three semibreves to the breve
and three minims to the semibreve. If the beat is on the minim in ₵ , it
would shift to the semibreve in (₵)2; if it is on the semibreve in O ,
it will remain there in (O)3.

         In O gemma lux and in Alma redemptoris we encounter for the first
time in the Dufay works the signature Ɔ , which has caused considerable

difficulty among theorists of the last five centuries. In these two works
it is found in the course of a section of ℂ and has the effect of replacing a semibreve of three minims by a breve of two semibreves, each semibreve containing two minims.

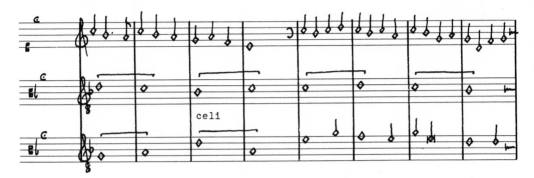

Musical Example 10: Dufay, _Alma_ _redemptoris_ (BU 64-65)

        Here we get to the root of one of the major confusions about the
matter of proportions. One way of looking at this relationship is that
three minims of ℂ are replaced by four minims of Ɔ , hence there is a
sesquitertia proportion.   Ɔ is one of the most ancient signatures, traceable well back into the fourteenth century, and its most usual meaning is
that employed by Dufay. Prosdocimus, writing a somewhat reactionary treatise in 1412, said, "Likewise there are some who would have the semicircle
open to the left, i.e., Ɔ , be the general sign showing us that we are to
sing the notes which follow in sesquitertia proportion (four to three, or
eight to six) to the notes in their normal value."[34]

        A fourteenth-century musician was expected to be able to deter-
mine the mensuration of a piece by scanning it, and composers of the time
rarely bothered to insert signatures which did nothing more than tell performers something they should have been able to figure out for themselves.
Signatures were used only when there was a change of mensuration within a
piece, or to show relationships which would not be clear otherwise. The
organization under Ɔ is the same as that under ℂ , with two semibreves
to the breve and two minims to the semibreve; but if a section in ℂ were
to follow ℂ there would be minim equivalence between the two, whereas a
section in Ɔ following ℂ would set up a 4:3 minim ratio, an unusual relationship which had to be shown by an unusual signature.

---

[34] Prosdocimus de Beldemanis, _Tractatus_ _practice_ _de_ _musica_ _mensurabili_,
in E. de Coussemaker (ed.), Scriptorum de musica medii aevi, III (Paris,
1864), p. 216.

The "classic" use of ⊃ was in relation to major prolation.
When ⊂ and ⊙ passed out of general usage, this signature fell into dis-
use, or misuse. Theorists, looking back at ancient music in which it was
found, could only see that it called for the replacement of a semibreve by
a breve; so it was classified as a sign of "duple" proportion. Since its
organization was the same as ⊂ , composers and theorists of the later fifteenth century sometimes used it as an equivalent of ¢ and ⊂ 2, both of
which were also thought of as calling for "diminution" of ⊂ .

Thus ⊃ following ⊂ calls for four minims to replace three,
but also for two semibreves to replace one. We have seen that the cipher
2 in the course of a section in ⊂ calls for two minims to replace one and
is therefore called a duple proportion—but it is also true that three
semibreves of (⊂)2 replace one of ⊂ , a triple proportion.

Besseler has a facsimile of the Velut ballade Laissies ester
facing page 128 of Bourdon und Fauxbourdon with the statement that this is
a "typisches Bild der Prolatio-Notierung." Albert Seay, in the preface to
his translation of the Tinctoris Proportionale Musices, says that by studying this treatise "the performer can gain an insight into the real nature
of this music, not the usual cliche that this is mathematical composition,
but the truer reaction that the composers of Tinctoris' time had discovered
something about the nature of polyrhythms which had been allowed to disappear all too soon."[35] Most textbooks on notation devote much of their
coverage of fifteenth-century practices to discussions of pieces making use
of a multiplicity of mensurations. All of this obscures the fact that the
"typical" piece from the first half of the century is in one of the basic
mensurations throughout, or alternates two or three of these if it is a
more extended composition. The flamboyant "polyrhythmic" pieces of Cordier,
Velut, Lebertoul, and Billart are found only in the seventh and eighth fascicles of Ox, all but two are unique to this manuscript, and they are clearly the product of a provincial group of composers whose work had little effect on the course of music outside their own circle.

There is no confusion on this point in the Dufay works of this
period. All proportions operate at the minim level and their nomenclature
refers to this level, no matter what relationships result at the other
levels of mensuration.

But there was no such uniformity in the works of certain other
composers. (See Musical Example 11.) Example 11, a transcription of the
first part of the anonymous Medee fut preserved in Ox, illustrates several
of the deviations from Dufay's simple, consistent usage found in the works

---

[35] Albert Seay, "The Proportionale Musices of Johannes Tinctoris," Journal
of Music Theory, 1 (1957), p. 24.

Canon: Ad figuram 3^{am} in proportione sesquialtera.
        Ad figuram 2^{am} in proportione sesquitertia.
        Ad figuram 4^{am} in proportione dupla.

Musical Example 11: anonymous, Medee fut (Ox 116'117)

Musical Example 11: completed

of his contemporaries. The piece begins in Ȼ , and the cipher 3 has the
effect of replacing two minims by three, just as in Dufay—though the latter
never used this cipher in Ȼ , only in O and C . The cipher 2, though,
calls for something quite different from what it does in the Dufay works:
one semibreve of Ȼ is replaced by two semibreves (of two minims each) of
(Ȼ)2, giving a relationship between the two mensurations correctly
labeled as sesquitertia by the accompanying canon, since four minims replace three. This is the relationship for which Dufay uses the signature
Ɔ . In this piece, then, the cipher 2 in the course of Ȼ refers to
semibreve, not minim, relationship. Later, the cipher 4 places two semibreves (of three minims each) where one semibreve (of three minims) had
been before, a relationship identified by the canon as a duple proportion
and one which has nothing to do with the figure 4. Thus, it is unnecessary
to examine stylistic features of this piece to know that it is not by Dufay
—mensural usage tells us this.

There is disagreement between the BU and Ox versions of La belle
se siet which falls in Group 2[a]: the piece is in Ȼ throughout in BU but
has alternate sections of Ȼ and (Ȼ)2 in Ox. An anonymous, three-voice
piece in BU, it is transposed in Ox, has three voices, and has an ascription to Dufay not at the beginning of the composition but over the contra
part, which is the voice not found in BU. It appears that Dufay reworked
a two-voice piece (from the nature of the music it could be a harmonization

of a folksong) into a three-voice composition. Example 12 is a transcription of the beginning of the two versions.

Musical Example 12: anonymous-Dufay, La belle se siet.

THE WORKS OF GROUP 2

1423-1429

Distinguishing characteristics: use of ₵ , C , and O as
basic mensureations; semibreve-minim movement in ₵ but a shift to breve-
semibreve movement in O and C ; flagged semiminims in ₵ , and either
no semiminims or a scattering of flagged semiminims in O and C .

Et in terra BL 138-139 - Patrem BL 140-142
   (₵) O ₵   (₵) O ₵

Et in terra BL 192   Apostolo glorioso
   (₵) O   (₵) O

Alma redemptoris mater BL 257   O gemma lux
  superius: (₵) Ɔ O ₵   superius: ₵ Ɔ₵2 ₵ Ɔ₵2 C
  T, CT: (₵) O ₵   T, CT: (₵)   C

Mon chier amy
  superius: (₵) 2 O 3 ₵ 2
  T, CT: (₵)   O   ₵

THE WORKS OF GROUP 2ᵃ
ca. 1415-1429

Distinguishing characteristics: use of ₵ with flagged semiminims, semibreve-minim movement.

Et in terra Ca6 24'27
(₵)

Belle plaissant   J'atendray tant
  (₵)   (₵)

Ce moys de may   J'ay grant desir
  (₵)   (₵)

Helas ma dame   Je me complains
  (₵)   (₵)

34

Je ne suy plus
   (₵)

La dolce vista
   (₵)

La belle se siet
₵ 2 ₵ 2 ₵ 2 ₵

Ma belle dame souverainne
   (₵)

THE WORKS OF GROUP 2[b]
1423-1433

Distinguishing characteristics: use of O or ₵ ; breve-semi-breve movement; no semiminims, or a scattering of flagged semiminims.

Et in terra MuEm 97'98
  (O)

Bon jour bon mois
  (O)

Alma redemptoris mater Tr92 178'179
  (O)

Dona i ardenti ray
  ₵

Anima mea
  (O)

Estrines moy
  (O)

Ave regina celorum BL 258
  (O)

He compaignons
  (O)

Gaude virgo
  (O)

Je ne puis plus
  (O)

Inclita stella maris
  ₵ / O

Portugaler
  (O)

Adieu ce bons vins
  (O)

Pour l'amour
  (O)

Bien veignes vous
  (O)

Quel fronte signorille
  (O)

CHAPTER 3
1426-1431

The Dufay motet <u>Rite maiorem</u>, in honor of St. James, was written in 1426 or 1427. Though it appears to be a five-voice composition, the contra part is a condensation of the tenor and solus tenor, and the piece can be performed as a four-voice composition by omitting the contra, or as a three-voice work by substituting the contra part for the two tenors. All voices begin in ₵, and change to O in the second part of the motet. Movement in ₵ is in semibreves and minims, and there is a shift to breve-semibreve movement in O. The piece seems to belong with the works of Group 2, with a fast beat on the minim in ₵ and a more moderate beat on the semibreve in O.

But a new signature is introduced: the superius twice changes to Φ, while the other voices continue in ₵. From a transcription we see that a semibreve of Φ is equivalent to a minim of ₵.

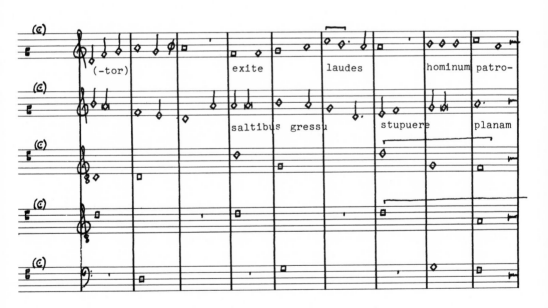

Musical Example 13: Dufay, <u>Rite maiorem</u> (BL 209)

Since in Φ the semibreve contains two minims and the breve three semibreves, and in C the minim contains two semiminims and the semibreve
three minims, this appears to be a genuine instance of a duple proportion
between two mensurations, at all levels.

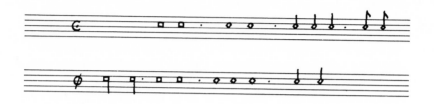

Musical Example 14: organization of C and Φ

        If the beat is on the minim in C, it must be on the semibreve
in Φ. All this is clear enough, and there remains only the question of
why Dufay used this new mensuration here. It appears that a change from
C to Φ would have no effect on the sound of the music, and in the transcription of this motet offered in the first volume of the Dufay Opera
Omnia, the shift has no effect on the appearance of the music; it is impossible to tell where the changes take place without consulting the critical notes.

        Besseler has suggested that Φ was used as a substitute for C,
around 1430, to allow for more ligatures. In pieces in C written at this
time the upper voices abound in semibreves and minims, usually with more
of the latter. Since there was no way to join minims together in ligatures,
or to join them to other notes, such parts contain almost no ligatures.
If the mensuration Φ is used as a replacement for C, however, minims become semibreves and semibreves become breves and there are many more oppor-
tunities for ligatures, particularly of the cum opposita proprietate variety. Besseler has detected a change to a more "cantabile" style of melodic
line around 1430, he interprets ligatures as signs of articulation, and he
believes that Φ was used in place of C to make more ligatures possible.

        But this explanation is not convincing for Rite maiorem, which is
one of the earliest Dufay works to make use of Φ. C.o.p. ligatures are by
no means abundant in the sections in Φ; there are only three of them, and
it is unlikely that Dufay changed mensuration for the sake of this handful
of ligatures.

        An alternate explanation is that the change from C to Φ brings
about a change in tempo. I have already called attention to several apparently identical mensurations which turn out to differ from one another in

tempo: O and (C)2 are organized in exactly the same way, for instance, but move at different tempi. I suggest that the signature Φ, as used in Rite maiorem, calls for a beat on the semibreve somewhat faster than the beat on the semibreve in O and somewhat slower than the beat on the minim in C. A count of notes used in each mensuration in this piece gives:

	longs	breves	semibreves	minims
C	-	16	62	70
O	1	17	81	66
Φ	-	14	36	30

Minims are the most frequently used notes in C, semibreves in O and Φ. A composer changing to a mensuration moving faster than the one he has been using will tend to use larger notes. This is not to suggest that Dufay himself kept track of the number of breves, semibreves, and minims he was using, but that he would vary the proportions of these instinctively in different mensurations. The number of breves in the sections of Rite maiorem in O is approximately a fourth of the number of minims, while in sections in Φ there are almost half as many breves as minims.

There is an obvious objection to the suggestion that C and Φ called for different tempi in Rite maiorem. With all voices in C at the beginning of the piece, the proper beat for this mensuration could be set by a musician singing from any one of the voice parts, but when the superius changes to Φ, the other voices continue in C; and if there were a change in the speed of the beat, it would have to come from someone singing or following the superius part, since there are no clues as to this tempo change in the other parts.

This is not a serious objection. Many of the paintings which give us information on musical practice of the fifteenth century show a boy giving the beat, suggesting that it was a menial task and that it was done by a singer who would probably be reading the superius part. And if the time-beater were not singing while performing his function, the logical voice for him to follow would be the top one on the page.

A more troublesome point is that if the speed of the beat were to be changed to accomodate the change to Φ, this new beat would then go at the wrong speed for the other voices still singing in C. But this objection is valid only if can be established that the speed of the beat remained constant in all mensurations in the first half of the fifteenth century. I have offered some evidence that this was not the case, and in the course of this book other evidence will be brought out to support my contention that the beat in the Dufay era, far from being invariable in speed, was subject to many gradations of tempo. In Rite maiorem the signature C informed the singers that they were to sing one minim to each beat, and that

the beat would be fast. If in the course of the piece the beat were to be
slowed down somewhat to accomodate another mensuration in another voice,
then brought back to its original speed, the singers would have no particular difficulty in continuing to sing one minim, or its equivalent, to each
of these beats, even if there was some slight change in rate of speed.

I suggest, then, that in Rite maiorem and in other works written
at this time, the beats for Ȼ and Ø were different enough in speed so
that when the two were used in consecutive sections of a composition there
would be a detectable difference in tempo, yet similar enough so that when
the two were used simultaneously they could be incorporated under the same
beat. I offer not as a guess to the absolute speed of the beat in these
mensurations but as a guess to the ratios between them:

> O beat on the semibreve, 75 beats per minute
> Ø beat on the semibreve, 100 beats per minute
> Ȼ beat on the minim,   125 beats per minute

There are pieces by composers other than Dufay in which sectional
use of Ȼ and Ø is explainable only as a tempo change between the two.
The Lymburgia Sanctus (BL 164) has the pattern ØOØOȻO in all voices.
Ox 104'105, an Et in terra by Le Grant Guillaume, has alternate sections in
Ȼ (for two voices) and Ø (for three voices); the following Patrem (Ox
105'107) by the same composer, dated 1426 in the manuscript, alternates
duet sections in Ȼ with trio sections in C. In the mass by Arnold de
Lantins, on the other hand, the use of Ȼ and Ø must be a chronological
matter. The Kyrie, Et in terra, and Patrem have alternating sections in Ȼ,
O, and C, while the Sanctus and Agnus Dei use Ø, O, and C. The first
three sections are grouped together in Ox and the other two are paired further along in the manuscript; the first three are found in BU, the last two
are not; the first three use flagged simiminims, the other two have colored
ones. Apparently, the Sanctus and Agnus Dei were written a few years after
the first three sections, and in the interim, the composer had abandoned Ȼ
in favor of Ø—and, incidentally, flagged semiminims for colored.

I have brought together as Group 3 all Dufay works which make use
of both Ȼ and Ø. The group is small and there is no difficulty in setting
up the years 1426-1431 as boundaries, since almost every piece can be dated
with some accuracy. Besseler has convinced almost everyone that the Missa
Sancti Jacobi dates from 1426-1427, and that the motet Rite maiorem was
written at the same time. Balsamus et munda and Ecclesie militantis have
both been given the date of 1431.[1] De Van suggested a date of 1437 for

---

[1] But see pp. 67 ff. for a discussion of the possibility that Ecclesie
militantis does not date from 1431.

O sancte Sebastiane:[2] the text is an invocation for protection from the
plague (there was an outbreak in Italy in 1437, and it was thought that
Dufay was in Bologna in this year). But nothing about the piece suggests
the kind of music Dufay wrote in the late 1430's, and Besseler's suggestion,
in "Dufay in Rom," that the motet was written in 1429 is much more satis-
factory. There was such a severe epidemic in Rome in this year that the
Pope fled the city; Dufay was there as a member of the Papal Choir.

Much has been written about the Missa Sancti Jacobi in recent
years because of the critical role it may have played in the history of
fauxbourdon. It also proves to be a useful work for tracing mensural practice in the 1420's, particularly the replacement of ₵ by Φ. The nine
sections of the mass are grouped together in BL in correct sequence, under
the title by which the work is known today. The five sections of the ordi-
mary are also found in Ao, though not in sequence, each section labeled "de
apostolis." None of the proper sections are found in this manuscript, and
if we had only this source for the work there would be no reason to connect
it with Saint James.

The first four sections of the ordinary have similar structure,
with alternation between "chorus" sections in ₵, "duo" sections in O,
and "chorus" sections in C. Movement in ₵ is in semibreves and minims,
with the latter in the majority, and there is a scattering of flagged semiminims. There is also semibreve-minim movement in O and C, but in these
mensurations there are more of the larger notes, and there are also relatively more breves than in major prolation. The following count is of the
first section of the Et in terra:

	longs	breves	semibreves	minims	semiminims
₵	3	20	75	79	2
O	2	20	64	36	-
C	3	23	79	32	-

On the basis of the first four sections of the ordinary, the mass
belongs in my Group 2. But the signature Φ is used in the second and
third section of the Agnus Dei and in each of the four proper sections.
These five parts are also quite different in organization from the first
four section of the ordinary, making no use of chorus-duo alternation, and
it is my guess that the latter were written first, probably before 1426,
and that the proper sections were added slightly later to make it a topical
mass.

The introitus begins in tempus perfectum, with no signature in
any of the four voices. There is a change to Ɔ in the two upper voices,

2 G. de Van, Opera Omnia, I. p. xiv.

followed by the signature Φ. The two lower voices have no change of mensuration; since there is equivalence between them and the upper voices when
the latter have an explicit signature of Φ, all voices must be in (Φ) at
the beginning. If I am correct in assuming that Φ called for a tempo different from ⊄ and O, it is strange that this tempo was not specified by
the proper signature at the beginning. This could have caused some slight
difficulty in a first reading of the piece, but only with the tempo, since
O and Φ are identical in organization.

    In earlier works, Dufay had used Ɔ in relation to major prola-
tion, to bring about a 4:3 ratio at the minim level. In this mass the signature causes the replacement of a breve (of three semibreves) in Φ by a
long (of two breves, each containing two semibreves). This could be thought
of as a duple proportion, since a long (of two breves) replaces a single
breve, but it is also true that three semibreves of Φ are replaced by four
of Ɔ. The function of Ɔ in relation to Φ is the same as its function in
relation to ⊄, but at the next level of mensuration—another clue that
Dufay thought of Φ and ⊄ as having a great deal to do with one another.

    In the offertory, <u>In omnem terram</u>, after sections in ⊄ and O,
three of the voices have Φ against ⊄ in the tenor, raising again the
question of why Dufay used two apparently equivalent mensurations, since
here also a semibreve of Φ corresponds to a minim of ⊄. The voices in Φ
are no more or less syllabic than they have been in the preceding sections
in ⊄ and O, and c.o.p. ligatures are not significantly abundant. Movement
in Φ is:

	longs	breves	semibreves	minims
Φ	8	18	59	27

If it is assumed that Φ is nothing more than ⊄ written at the next level
of mensuration, we see that if this section had been in ⊄ there would have
been 27 semiminims, almost a fourth of all of the notes. In no Dufay piece
is the percentage of semiminims anywhere near this great. I have suggested
that the signature Φ was a tempo indication, calling for a somewhat slower
beat on the semibreve than that on the minim in ⊄; this difference in the
speed of the beat might be reflected by the larger percentage of notes of
the smallest value found in sections written in the mensuration calling for
the slower beat.

    The tenor, in ⊄, moves in breves and longs. If it had been
written in Φ, like the other parts, its movement would have been in longs
and maxims. Even though musicians of the time supposedly knew the values
of such notes in the various mensurations, they almost never encountered
them. The use of ⊄ in the tenor part of a piece otherwise in Φ made it
possible for this voice to be written in notes half the value of those which
would have been necessary if it too had been in Φ.

A few decades after this, when major prolation was no longer in general use, the signature Ↄ was used in tenor parts of tenor masses, to prolong the cantus firmus. The usage in In omnem terram and in many other pieces from the same period is quite different: Ↄ is behaving normally, with each minim sung to one fast beat, and this mensuration is equated with tempus perfectum by having the latter move along somewhat faster than usual, i.e., by altering it to tempus perfectum diminutum. This earlier practice, for which I will coin the term "pseudo-augmentation," has been confused with genuine augmentation of a slightly later period.

Many compositions of this time by composers other than Dufay exhibit the same practice of indicating that tempus perfectum is to be "diminished" when used simultaneously with Ↄ. For example:

Ox 97, Je ne vis pas by R. Gallo, is written for two voices in Ↄ. A triplum part by Francus de Insula, apparently added later, begins in Φ;

BL 161, a Lymburgia Kyrie, has ΦOΦ in the superius against ↃOↃ in the tenor and contra;

BL 162, a Lymburgia Et in terra, has ΦOΦ in all parts but the contra, which has ΦOↃ;

BL 239, the motet Carminibus festos by Anthonius Romanus dating from 1423, has two upper voices in ΦCΦC against a tenor and contra in ↃOↃO;

BL 278, Pondelly's Verbum tuum, has a scheme of OↃCↃ in the superius against OↃCΦ in the other voices;

Ox 21', Se liesse est by J. Legrant, has a tenor and contra in Ↄ against a superius in tempus perfectum with a signature of 2 indicating that it is to be diminished;

Ox 108', Cordier's Pour le deffault, has a signature of O2 in the superius against the mensuration of Ↄ in the two lower voices; and

Ox 120'121, Prophetarum fulti by Grenon, has a section in which the superius has O2 against Ↄ in the tenor.

In each of these pieces the diminution of tempus perfectum is made explicit by a signature of either Φ or O2. There are also pieces with one or more voices in tempus perfectum, but with no signature, which work only if diminution is assumed. Among these are:

BL 256, the Grenon motet Plasmatoris humani. The two upper voices are in tempus perfectum with no signature, the other two voices have a signature of Ↄ. Later in the piece the signature O is found in all voices. Signatures were never found in the course of a composition from this period unless they were necessitated by a change in mensuration; so the upper voices must have begun in (Φ). Transcription shows that a semibreve of this mensuration equals a minim of Ↄ.

BL 252, <u>Aurea</u> <u>flamigeri</u> by Anthonius Romanus. All four voices begin in tempus perfectum, with no signature. In the course of the piece the superius changes to Ɔ , then to Ȼ, the notetus changes to Ȼ, and the tenor and contra continue in tempus perfectum. Since a minim of Ȼ in the top voices equals a semibreve in the lower, the piece must begin in— and the lower voices continue in—(Φ).

BL 272, <u>Ducales</u> <u>sedes</u> by Anthonius Romanus. The two upper voices are in tempus perfectum, with no signature, against Ȼ in the contra and tenor; they must be in (Φ). This motet is found in a three-voice version on BU 76-77, with all voices in Ȼ.

BL 253, <u>Dominicus</u> <u>a</u> <u>dono</u> by Christoforus de Monte. The two top voices are in tempus perfectum with no signature, and the presence of Ȼ in the tenor and contra makes it clear that they must be in (Φ).

Tr92 128'130, an anonymous <u>Et</u> <u>in</u> <u>terra</u>. The two upper voices are in tempus perfectum with no signature, but the tenor mensuration of (Ȼ) is the clue that they must be in (Φ).

In still other pieces, transcription reveals that a mensuration of Φ is intended even though it is not made explicit by a signature. BL 242, Grenon's <u>Ad</u> <u>honorem</u>, has all four voices in tempus perfectum at the beginning, without signature but with the canon "ut iacet" for tenor and contra; the second part has Φ for all voices. The beginning can be transcribed only if (Φ) is assumed for the top voices against the tempus perfectum "ut iacet" (i.e., O) of the other two. Ox 108, the anonymous <u>Il</u> <u>n'est</u> <u>dangier</u>, also starts with tempus perfectum with no signature, in all voices; the superius changes to Ɔ, then to Φ, and since this latter section is equivalent to the tempus perfectum of the other voices, which have not changed mensuration, all voices must be in (Φ) at the beginning.

Since tempus perfectum in these pieces turns out to be (Φ), it is possible that other works in this mensuration, without signature, were also intended to be in (Φ) rather than (O). Some scholars have assumed this: <u>Flos</u> <u>florum</u> and <u>Ave</u> <u>virgo</u> <u>que</u> <u>de</u> <u>celis</u> are printed in the Dufay <u>Opera</u> <u>Omnia</u> in "tempus perfectum diminutum," the editor explaining that this mensuration was "suggested by the notation";[3] and Besseler, in "Dufay in Rom" and elsewhere suggests (Φ) for entire groups of compositions.

It has been assumed that movement in (Φ) is in larger notes than in (O), and this has been the basis for the detection of undesignated (Φ). Certainly there are pieces in tempus perfectum with breve-semibreve movement which contrast with the normal semibreve-minim movement in this mensuration. For example, Ox 61', an <u>Et</u> <u>in</u> <u>terra</u> by Hugo de Lantins, moves almost entirely

---

[3] <u>Ibid</u>., p. xx.

in breves and semibreves, with only two minims in the entire composition.
It is in tempus perfectum with no signature, but the scribe has grouped the
Et in terra's in the index and in many cases referred to them by signature,
to differentiate one from another—and he gives a signature of Φ for this
piece.

This suggests that such a piece as the Dufay _Anima mea_, with a
mensuration of tempus perfectum, no signature, and movement mostly in breves
and semibreves, was thought of as being in (Φ). But even though Dufay's
Alma redemptoris Tr92 178'179 and _Ave regina_ (BL 258) also move in breves
and semibreves, the former has a signature of O in Tr92 and the latter has
the same in Ox. In my opinion, Φ should be reserved for those pieces which
have such a signature and those in which it is demanded by the context.

A count of the two upper voices of the Grenon _Plasmatoris humani_
gives:

	longs	breves	semibreves	minims
(Φ)	27	121	310	117

and a count of the superius of the Dufay _Alma redemptoris_, in tempus perfectum with no signature, gives:

longs	breves	semibreves	minims
9	76	90	38

Movement in the Dufay piece is much more decidedly in breves and semibreves
than in the Grenon motet, and since the latter has a signature of Φ, it
might be assumed that it is also in this mensuration. But the manuscript
gives a signature of O.

A count of the notes in a composition from this period with sections in both O and Φ will usually reveal a shift to larger notes in the
latter, but this shift is so slight as to be undetectable without such a
count and could not have been apparent to a musician performing the piece.
And there is considerable variation in the ratios between the various notes
in O and Φ from composer to composer, and even from piece to piece by the
same composer. It is not possible to detect unspecified use of Φ by a
comparison with other pieces in which the signature is given.

In each of the pieces mentioned thus far in which tempus perfectum is used simultaneously with ℂ, there is either a signature of Φ or
O2 signaling diminution, or there is no signature; in neither case is the
Φ demanded by the context contradicted by another signature. But OH 93'94,
a _Sanctus_ by Leonel Power, is more troublesome. The mensuration pattern is:

superius, contra: (O) ℂ O
tenor: (ℂ) ℂ ℂ

A semibreve of the upper voices equals a minim of the tenor in the first
section, just as in the pieces described above, and as before we can assume
that the top parts are in (Φ). Attempts at transcription of the last section, however, lead to the discovery that here, too, a semibreve of the
upper parts equals a minim of the tenor, and in this case we cannot assume
the presence of (Φ) in the top voices because they are clearly furnished
with the signature O.

            One explanation for this situation is that we have here a prac-
tice differing from that of Dufay and other continental composers: a voice
in C against other parts in tempus perfectum must adjust to the more moderate beat prevailing in O rather than requiring the latter mensuration to
submit to "diminution" to bring it in line with the faster beat in C.
Another possibility, however, is that C and O were normally in proportion
to one another in English music of this time, with a minim of the former
equaling a semibreve of the latter.

            Curiously, the middle section of the Leonel piece can be tran-
scribed only if a minim of the tenor, which has a signature of C, is assumed to be equal to a semibreve of the upper parts, which also are in C.
Closer examination of OH reveals that signatures of Φ and ¢ are nowhere
to be found, even though a number of pieces seem to demand these signatures,
by their mensural context. Both suggestions offered in the previous para-
graph must be rejected; the situation can be explained more easily as resulting from curious deficiencies in the notation.

            In this piece by Leonel, then, either the tenor is in augmentation
in all three sections, or the two upper voices are to be diminished throughout. OH 17'18, another Leonel Et in terra with a similar three-part structure, contains a clue suggesting that the latter is the case. The first
section has (C) in the tenor against tempus perfectum in the superius and
contra, with no signature. There is a change to Ɔ in the superius, with
the other voices continuing in their original mensurations, and the effect
of this signature is to replace a breve of three semibreves by a long of
two breves, each breve containing two semibreves. This is the same relationship between Φ and Ɔ found in the introit of Dufay's Missa Sancti
Jacobi, and in the works of many composers of the time Ɔ is used only in
relation to C or Φ, never O.

            Semiminims in the Power Et in terra are colored, not flagged,
which leads to perhaps the strongest argument for considering the voices in
tempus perfectum against C as being in diminution, as in the Dufay works.
The superius of the first section of OH 68'69, a Leonel Power Patrem, has a
pattern of (O) Ɔ O against an unchanging mensuration of C in the contra;
a minim of C equals a semibreve of tempus perfectum, suggesting that the top
voice is in (Φ), as does the use of Ɔ. But when the entire piece is
transcribed, we discover that the section of the superius following the

passage in Ɔ, explicitly marked O, is equivalent in mensuration to the
section in tempus perfectum before the Ɔ ; so the piece must begin in (O),
in the superius. The composition is furnished with a canon to help the
singer over some of the notational hurdles, reading in part: "In proportione
dupla generat hic ♩." Colored semiminims are used here, then, to signal that
the mensuration in which they are found is to be subjected to diminution;
this signal is found only in sections in tempus perfectum occurring simultaneously with the mensuration ℭ, and it is used not only where there is
no signature, but also in sections which already have a signature of O.

Thus the clues which enable us to detect the mensuration (Φ) in
other sources are valid for OH also, even though certain passages which we
can furnish with (Φ) already have the signature O.

There is further evidence of the English avoidance of the signature Φ in this manuscript. OH 84', an anonymous <u>Sanctus</u>, has a final section marked with O, with the modification "per dimidietatem." OH 92', a
<u>Sanctus</u> by Sturgeon, begins in tempus perfectum with no signature; a second
section follows, with the signature O and the instruction "sicut jacet"
which makes it clear that the piece began in (Φ).

I have found seven pieces in OH in which tempus perfectum is diminished by the presence of ℭ in another voice:

OH 17'18	Leonel	<u>Et in terra</u>
OH 19'20	(Leonel)	<u>Et in terra</u>
OH 60'61	Damett	<u>Patrem</u>
OH 68'69	Leonel	<u>Patrem</u>
OH 69'70	(Leonel)	<u>Patrem</u>
OH 70'71	Leonel	<u>Patrem</u>
OH 93'94	Leonel	<u>Sanctus</u>

It is striking that six of the seven are by Leonel Power. This same device,
pseudo-augmentation, is found in Power works preserved in other manuscripts
and also in pieces by such slightly younger English composers as Forest and
Dunstable. I have already called attention to the use of the device by continental composers active in the first third of the century, and there can
be no mistaking the fact that Leonel played an important liason role between
English and continental music. Almost half of the English pieces in OH
found in continental manuscripts are by him.

It seems unlikely that Leonel himself originated the practice of
pseudo-augmentation. We know little about him beyond the fact that he died
in 1445,[4] and with this single date to go on, it is risky to guess at an
approximate date of birth. Pseudo-augmentation can be traced back to 1414

---

[4] Frank L. Harrison, <u>Music in Medieval Britian</u> (London, 1958).

on the Continent, in the motet <u>Ducales</u> <u>sedes</u> by Anthonius Romanus; Leonel
may not have been writing music this early. Contact between English and
continental musicians could have taken place during the Council of Constance
(1414-1418), but we have no evidence that Leonel Power was in attendance.
It is unnecessary to assume personal contact between composers for the device of pseudo-augmentation to have been passed from one to another, nor
could it have been detected from a hearing of a piece in which it was used.
If Power learned it from Italian music, this could have been done from a
manuscript studied in the comfort of his home in England.

   I suggest, then, that in the first third of the fifteenth century
the presence of one or more voices in ₵(or, rarely, ☉) against one or
more voices in tempus perfectum called for diminution of the voices in the
latter mensurations, whether the composer of the piece was French, English,
or Italian. I have repeatedly suggested that the beat in ₵ at this time
was on the minim, and that it was a fast beat; that ○ was beat on the semibreve, at a more moderate rate of speed; and that the fast beat in ₵ was
not in a 2:1 ratio to the slower one in ○. Thus the diminution resulting
from the adjustment of the beat in tempus perfectum to the faster beat in
₵ was not diminution by half, but merely an increase in tempo. If it had
been by half, we would expect to find some shift in note values to compensate for the doubling of the tempo, a shift from the normal semibreve-minim
movement in ○ towards breve-semibreve movement. The count of the Dufay
<u>Rite</u> <u>maiorem</u> (p. 39) shows that this is not the case, as does a comparison
of movement in Φ in the offertory of the <u>Missa</u> <u>Sancti</u> <u>Jacobi</u> (p.42) with
movement in ○ in the <u>Et</u> <u>in</u> <u>terra</u> of the same mass (p.41). Nor do we find
such a shift in pieces by Leonel Power. The superius of the first section
of his <u>Patrem</u> OH 68'69, marked with a signature of ○ but to be read in
diminution, moves:

	<u>longs</u>	<u>breves</u>	<u>semibreves</u>	<u>minims</u>	<u>semiminims</u>
○ (= Φ)	7	21	86	85	10

His <u>Sanctus</u> OH 94'95 also has a first section with a signature of ○, with
no reason in this case to suspect Φ; movement is:

	<u>longs</u>	<u>breves</u>	<u>semibreves</u>	<u>minims</u>	<u>semiminims</u>
○	2	36	66	68	-

   In each of the pieces listed and discussed above, in which ₵ and
tempus perfectum are used simultaneously, ₵ is found in the tenor and/or
contra part. In the Leonel Power <u>Et</u> <u>in</u> <u>terra</u> (OH 19'20) all voices begin
in (₵), then the tenor and contra change to ○ against continuation of
major prolation in the superius, bring about a situation just the reverse
of usual. Just at the point where the lower voices change to tempus perfectum, there is semibreve coloration in the (₵) of the superius.

Musical Example 15:   Leonel Power, Et in terra (OH 19'20)

Three colored semibreves of two minims each in (C) equal three normal semibreves of two minims each in O. The two mensurations are not equivalent,
however: each breve in (C) contains two semibreves, as opposed to three
in O, and a "Grosstakt" of six semibreves results. The most interesting
point, however, is the minim equivalence between (C) and O. Later in this
same piece, C in the tenor against tempus perfectum in the other voices results in pseudo-augmentation, with the usual relationship of a minim of C
equalling a semibreve of (Φ). Thus we see in this piece a practice which
was to become a convention later in the century: C in the tenor, or in a
part performing the function of the tenor, against tempus perfectum signals
a proportional relationship between the two mensurations, but if C is found
in a part other than the tenor against O in one or more of the other voices,
there is minim equivalence.

The Power Missa alma redemptoris preserved in Tr87 and Ao is
thought to be one of the very earliest tenor masses. We have no clue as to
the date of the piece beyond the fact that it must have been written before
1445, the year of the composer's death. The tenor is in C for the first
part of each section, the other voices are in tempus perfectum with no signature, and it has been assumed that this is an early example of augmentation effected by the use of major prolation in the tenor. Since this combination of mensurations in earlier works by Leonel—assuming that the OH
repertoire is older than this mass—results in pseudo-augmentation, would
not the same be true here?

Besseler has suggested that the beat slowed down around 1430, on
the basis of his ability to scan a piece of music and sense how fast it
should move to make the best musical sense, and this suggestion is supported
by counts of movement in pieces falling on either side of 1430. A count of
two Leonel pieces in tempus perfectum has been given above, and if we accept
the current opinion on the date of OH,[5] we can place them before 1430. In

———————
[5] M. Bukofzer, Studies in Medieval and Renaissance Music (New York, 1950),
pp. 73-80.

these and in other pieces by Leonel, movement in O is in semibreves and
minims, with approximately the same number of each. But a count of this
same mensuration in the Missa alma redemptoris reveals a different situation, with movement still in semibreves and minims but with the latter decidedly in the majority. This count is of the first section of the Et in
terra:

	longs	breves	semibreves	minims	semiminims
(O)	1	13	55	112	13

The same shift toward smaller notes can be seen in the Dufay
works. In pieces written in the 1420's, movement in C is in semibreves
and minims, with just about as many of one as the other. Around 1430,
however, the ratio between the two becomes quite unbalanced in favor of
the latter:

	longs	breves	semibreves	minims	semiminims
Rite maiorem (1426)	-	16	62	70	-
Et in terra (MSJ) (ca. 1426)	6	32	150	137	2
O sancte Sebastiane (1429)	1	23	165	278	-
Balsamus et munda (1431)	-	6	80	190	41

A similar shift to smaller notes can be seen in the mensuration
Φ, showing up most clearly in the ratio between breves and minims:

	longs	breves	semibreves	minims	semiminims
Rite maiorem (1426)	-	14	36	30	-
In omnem terram (1426-27)	8	18	59	27	-
O sancte Sebastiane (1429)	8	39	195	169	-
Balsamus et munda (1431)	2	14	76	65	-

On the basis of this series of observations, I suggest the following chronology for the origin of pseudo-augmentation and its subsequent
alteration into true augmentation.

1. In the 1420's, and possibly earlier, there was a fast beat on
the minim in major prolation and a more moderate beat on the semibreve in
minor prolation.

2. These two beats, while clearly different in speed, were yet similar enough to make it possible for major and minor prolation to occur simultaneously, with a minim—i.e., one beat—of the former equaling a semibreve—i.e., one beat—of the latter. Some composers used a signature of Φ or O2 to show that in this situation the voices in minor prolation were to move more rapidly than usual, to bring the speed of the beat nearer that prevailing in major prolation. Other composers regarded the mere fact that the two mensurations were used against one another as enough of a signal that a faster beat was required.

3. Around 1430, the beat in the various mensurations became slower.

4. Around 1430, most composers abandoned major prolation. In the following decades it was used only in certain exceptional compositions, and performance practice relating to ℂ was gradually forgotten.[6] The most common signatures just after the abandonment of ℂ were O, C, and Φ, and in each of these the beat was on the semibreve.

5. Theorists, themselves removed from performance practice, began assuming that the beat on the semibreve was the norm for all mensurations.

6. After 1430, major prolation (ℂ or ⊙) was sometimes used in the tenor and/or contra part of a motet or mass as an artificial signature. The beat was intended to fall on the minim and, being determined by the mensuration of the other voices, was the moderately slow beat prevailing at the time. Since the beat was now thought of as falling normally on the semibreve, the situation of having a beat on the minim in the tenor was thought of as augmentation; and since the beat on the minim in ℂ was a much slower one than had been used when this was a common signature, there was also augmentation in relation to this older practice.

MuEm 1 is a brief piece, ascribed to "Dufay," with a text in the top voice beginning "Qui latuit in virgine"; the other two voices are textless. The piece is also found in Tr87 109, anonymous and textless except for a text incipit "Du pist mein Hort" in the tenor. De Van has printed the piece in the first volume of the Dufay Opera Omnia with the suggestion that "the motet was composed by some German musician for instruments alone."[7] But certain clues in the Trent source enable us to make a more informed guess as to who might have written the piece.

---

[6] Tr88 is one of the later of this group of codices, dating probably from the 1460's or 1470's. Tr88 384'386, a Dufay Et in terra, is an early work fitting in my Group 2. The first section is in ℂ and the scribe, uncertain of the singers' ability to apply the rules of alteration in this mensuration, has put a small figure 2 under each minim which is to be altered.

[7] G. de Van Opera Omnia, I, p. xxii.

The top voice in MuEm has a signature of Φ, the other two voices are in tempus perfectum with no signature. In Tr87, however, the two upper voices are in tempus perfectum with no signature while the tenor is in (℃). The superius has the direction "trebulus per diminutionem," the next voice "contra per diminutionem," and the tenor "sicut jacet"; thus the piece is a good example of pseudo-augmentation, with the voices in tempus perfectum given an explicit direction to go faster than would have been normal in this mensuration, to compensate for the presence of major prolation in the tenor.[8]

A curious feature of the piece is that colored semiminims are used in the upper voices, but the single semiminim in the tenor is of the flagged type. The "trebulus" voice has a peculiar passage using both a cipher 3 and coloration.

Musical Example 16: Dufay-anonymous, textless piece (Tr87 109)

Even though the 3 is not canceled by a succeeding signature, it applies only to the brief section in coloration. Nor are the 3 and the coloration redundant: the former operates at the minim level, giving three minims in the time of two; the latter is semibreve coloration, putting three in place of two. This brief melodic turn is so characteristic of English composers, from Leonel Power to Bedingham, that its presence in a piece must raise the strong suspicion that it was written by an Englishman. Variations of this "English figure" are given in Musical Example 17.

Tr 87 117'118 is a companion piece: it is for three voices, the top two in tempus perfectum with the direction "per diminutionem" to accomodate a mensuration of ℃ in the tenor; the upper voices have colored semiminims, as opposed to the flagged ones of the tenor; the piece is textless; it appears to be inserted in the manuscript in the same hand which

---

[8] Bukofzer, in "Changing Aspects of Medieval and Renaissance Music," MQ, 44, (1958), 15-16, identifies the tenor as the basse dance Je suis si pauvre de liesse.

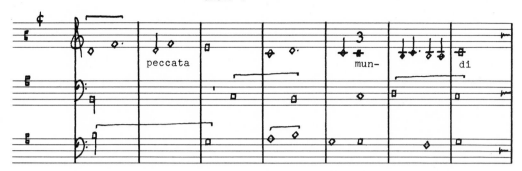

Musical Example 17: anonymous <u>Et in terra</u> (Tr90 117'118)

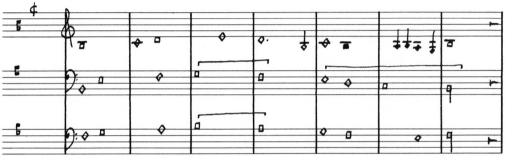

Dunstable-Leonel, <u>Et in terra</u> (Tr92 144'145)

copied <u>Qui latuit</u>. Bukofzer noted resemblances between the tenor and the <u>basse dance Aux ce bon yome</u> found in the Digby manuscript.[9]

The textless piece Tr87 118 belongs with these two. Again the upper voice is a "trebulus," and the English figure, notated with both coloration and the cipher 3, occurs in this voice. All three voices are in ₵, with movement predominantly in minims and (flagged) semiminims, in contrast to the normal semibreve-minim movement found in this mensuration.

In these three pieces, colored semiminims are used in minor prolation and flagged ones in major, the latter form apparently signaling that some type of augmentation is to take place. The use of flagged semiminims as a signal is yet another clue that these works are English, this practice being traceable to certain other compositions of the time attributed to English composers.

1. Dunstable's <u>Quam pulchra es</u> has a first section in tempus perfectum with semibreve-minim movement, simiminims being of the colored type. The second section is in ₵, with minim-semiminim movement and flagged semiminims. Bukofzer calls attention to the fact that the contrast

---

[9] <u>Ibid</u>., p. 16.

in semiminim type is observed in all sources[10] and quite properly transcribes the second part in note values twice as large as those he used for
the first section.

2. Tr92 104'105, a setting of Tota pulchra es by Forest, has a
mensuration pattern of O C O in all voices. The first and last sections
move in semibreves and minims, with a scattering of colored semiminims,
while the middle section has minim-semiminim movement, with flagged semiminims which apparently signal augmentation.

3. Tr92 171'172, an Ave regina by Leonel Power, has a section
in C with semibreve-minim movement and a few colored semiminims, then a
section in C moving in minims and flagged semiminims.

4. Tr 92 115'116, a Forest Patrem, has the scheme (O) C O in
the superius against C C C in the tenor and contra. From a transcription,
we see that the tenor and contra are in augmentation throughout, or else
the superius is in diminution, since a semibreve of the upper voice equals
a minim of the other voices in all three sections. The top voice has
colored semiminims throughout, the tenor and contra flagged ones; augmentation of the lower voices rather than diminution of the top part is intended.

Having suggested that the textless piece on Tr87 118 is English,
I will further point out that it must be a carol. The end of the burden
is marked off by pauses and two-breve rests in each voice part, and there
is the suggestion of a brief recapitulation of the burden at the end of
the verse. A transcription of the piece is found in an article of mine in
Music and Letters.[11]

We can add to our group the anonymous, textless three-voice composition Tr87 119, which is copied in the same fascicle in the same hand,
has a "trebulus" voice on top, and is written in C with all voices moving
in minims and (flagged) semiminims. The piece is copied into the manuscript twice, in slightly different versions.

Further along in the same manuscript, in the same hand, is still
another textless, three-voice piece (Tr87 198'199), with the "trebulus"
and contra in tempus perfectum, using colored semiminims, and the tenor in
major prolation. Both upper voices use the English figure mentioned above.

---

[10] M. Bukofzer (ed.), John Dunstable: Complete Works, p. 182. He is not
quite accurate, however: the BU version has flagged semiminims in both
mensurations.

[11] C. Hamm, "A Group of Anonymous English Pieces in Trent 87," M&L, 41
(1960), pp. 214-215. Brian Trowell offers several corrections in the
following issue.

This piece is not anonymous, however, being attributed to "Tyling," a name which could well be English.[12]

A final piece can be added to our group, Tr87 199'200. It is textless, written for "trebulus" and two other voices, and has Ȼ in all voices with movement in minims and (flagged) semiminims. The ascription is to "T," or possibly "TL."

These six pieces are in the same hand, copied into two fascicles of the manuscript. From all appearances they were added to the manuscript at the same time. They have certain peculiarities of mensural usage and are the only pieces in this part of the manuscript to have these. All six, including the one attributed to Dufay elsewhere, must be English. They may all be by Tyling, whoever he was.

---

[12] Bukofzer, in "Changing Aspects of Medieval and Renaissance Music," pp. 16-17, tentatively identifies the tenor as the Dutch popular song "T'Andernaken"—which, however, turns up in other English pieces. Cf. London, British Museum MS. add. 31922, 82'83, a three-voice piece with the inscription "The King. h. VII" and a textless tenor labeled "Tannder Naken."

THE WORKS OF GROUP 3
1426-1431

Distinguishing characteristics: use of both ₵ and Φ, flagged
semiminims.

Missa Sancti Jacobi

    Introit: superius   (Φ) ⊃ Φ ₵ ₵
             motetus   (Φ) ⊃ Φ
             tenor, contra   (Φ)   ₵ ₵
    Kyrie: (₵) O ₵ ₵ O ₵ ₵ O ₵
    Gloria: ₵ O ₵ ₵ O ₵
    Alleluia: (Φ) O Φ O
    Credo: (₵) O ₵ ₵ O ₵ ₵ O ₵ ₵ O
    Offertory: superius   ₵ ⊃ O Φ
               contra, tenor ₵   O Φ
    Sanctus: (₵) O ₵ O ₵ O
    Agnus Dei: ₵ Φ Φ
    Communion: (O)

Balsamus et munda   Rite maiorem
    superius, motetus: (₵) ⊃ Φ ₵ ⊃ Φ   superius: (₵) Φ ₵ Φ O
    contra: ⊙   others: ₵   O
    tenor: (by canon)

Ecclesie militantis   *Qui latuit
    triplum, motetus: (Φ) ¢ Φ   superius, contra: (Φ)
    contra: Φ   ¢ 3 Φ   tenor: ₵
    tenors: ₵ ¢ ₵ ¢ O Φ

O sancte Sebastiane   Belle vueillies may retenir
    superius, motetus: ₵ ⊃ ₵ ⊃ ₵ ⊃ Φ   Φ
    contra, tenor: ⊙   Φ

*
  Erroneously ascribed to Dufay.

CHAPTER 4
1426-1433

Dufay's first use of the signature Φ was in 1426-1427 in the
later sections of his Missa Sancti Jacobi, as well as I can determine,
though it had been used in pieces written well before this date by other
composers. Any Dufay work using this signature and making use of flagged
semiminims, which are not found in any of his works written after 1433,
must therefore fall in the period 1426-1433. All such pieces I have
brought together in Group 4.

These works were written in the same period as those of Group 3
and have many notational similarities with them, the only distinction being
that Group 3 contains works in which both Ȼ and Φ are used, whereas the
compositions in Group 4 do not make use of major prolation. Since the
latter mensuration was being abandoned by Dufay at just this time, most of
the pieces in Group 4 probably date from a few years later than most of
those in Group 3. The two datable works bear this out: Supremum est mortalibus celebrates the treaty between Pope Eugene IV and emperor-elect
Sigismund, signed on April 8 of 1433; and Besseler believes that C'est bien
raison, written for Nicholas III of Ferrara, dates from this same year.

The compositions of this group were written at about the period
when the type of semiminim used by Dufay was changing from flagged to
colored, and of the handful of pieces of which two or more manuscripts are
in disagreement as to type of semiminim, two (Supremum est and O beate
Sebastiane) fall in the present small group.

The only new signature found in this group is ȼ3, used for the
middle section of Supremum est.[1] The first and last sections of the piece
are in Φ, which has exactly the same organization as ȼ3: the breve has
three semibreves, the semibreve two minims. There must be some difference
between the two (even though they are transcribed in identical fashion in
the motet volume of the Opera Omnia), and the only possible difference is

---

[1] De Van reports on p. xvii of the preface to the second fascicle of
motets in the Dufay Opera Omnia that BL and MuEm have a signature of 4/3
at this point, adding that "4/3 = ȼ3." BL can, and should, be read as
ȼ3, with the 3 under the ȼ rather than after it. There is no 4:3 ratio,
at any level of mensuration, between the first and second parts of the
piece.

in tempo. A count of the two shows that there is semibreve-minim movement
in ϕ, as usual, but breve-semibreve movement in $\mathcal{C}$3:

	longs	breves	semibreves	minims	semiminims
ϕ	4	31	138	82	5
$\mathcal{C}$3	10	48	69	17	-

In earlier works, Dufay used the cipher 3 in the mensurations O
and C to put three minims in place of the normal two. If the beat was on
the semibreve in these two mensurations, as I have suggested, another inter-
pretation of the cipher could be that it causes three notes of equal duration to fall under one beat. In Supremum est its function is to put three
semibreves in the place of two in $\mathcal{C}$. Anticipating a bit, the signature $\mathcal{C}$
called for the beat to fall on the breve. If that is the case here, Dufay's
usage is perfectly consistent, since the 3 calls for three notes—semibreves,
in this case—of equal duration to fall under one beat.

A discussion of relative tempi in section of ϕ and $\mathcal{C}$3 must be
deferred until the troublesome matter of the proper tempo for ϕ itself has
been clarified. This mensuration is referred to in all twentieth-century
literature as "tempus perfectum diminutum," and most editors of fifteenth-
century music assume diminution by half. De Van and Besseler, in the Dufay
Opera Omnia, reduce note values in their transcriptions of pieces in ϕ (or
sections of works with this signature) by half, a semibreve of O being a
quarter note but a semibreve of ϕ becoming an eighth note. With no tempo
indication given to modify this relationship, a performance from such a
transcription will have sections in ϕ moving along twice as fast as those
in O. Besseler followed this same practice in his edition of Vergene
bella,[2] as do most of the editors of publications of the American Institute
of Musicology.

The word "diminutum" itself should cast doubt on this. The adjec-
tive dimidius, a, um means halved or divided into two equal parts, true
enough, but it is not the word in question. "Diminutum" is from diminutio,
-onis, a variant of the feminine noun deminutio, -onis, meaning a diminution, abatement or lessening with no connotation whatsoever that such de-
crease is by half.

Nor does the music using ϕ suggest diminution by half in relation
to O. A count of sections in O and ϕ in the Dufay Vergene bella gives:

---

[2] H. Besseler, "Guillaume Dufay: Zwölf geistliche und weltliche Werke,"
Das Chorwerk, 19 (1932), pp. 7-10.

	longs	breves	semibreves	minims	semiminims
Φ	8	37	96	115	4
O	1	11	33	33	-

In each, movement is in semibreves and minims, with approximately a third as many breves as minims. If the tempo relationship between the two were anything approaching 2:1, this should show up as some difference in movement in the two mensurations.

Testing a piece by another composer in the same way, we see that movement in the Lymburgia Patrem (BL 122-123) is:

	longs	breves	semibreves	minims	semiminims
O	4	114	388	184	4
Φ	-	87	257	143	3

This piece is found in the same section of BL as the Dufay piece, it has the same notational characteristics—consecutive use of O and Φ, flagged semiminims, avoidance of major prolation—and it would seem to date from just about the same time as Vergene bella. As in the Dufay work, there is no evidence that O and Φ were thought of as being in a 2:1 proportion to one another. Reducing the above count to percentages shows even more clearly how similar is the movement in the two:

	longs	breves	semibreves	minims	semiminims
O	0.6	16.4	55.9	26.5	0.6
Φ	-	17.6	52.2	29.0	1.2

Given two mensurations, one moving twice as fast as the other, one would expect similar cadential figures to use notes twice as large in the faster mensuration. Later, in a discussion of the relationship between the mensurations O and ₵, examples of such a situation will be given. But nothing of the sort shows up in a comparison of cadences in O and Φ. The superius part of all cadences in the Lymburgia Patrem (BL 122-123) are given in musical example 18, from which it can be seen that cadences of the same types, with notes of the same value, are found in the two.[3]

Example 19 is a transcription of two cadences from Dufay's Vergene bella, the first from a section in Φ and the second from O. Melodic figuration in the superius, approaching the cadence, is similar in the two.

---

[3] A characteristic of Lymburgia's style can be noted in these cadences: of the twenty found in this piece, only two are identical, the third and the ninth in O. This undoubtedly deliberate varying of melodic detail contrasts with the practice of other composers of the time who were content to repeat stereotyped melodic formulae at cadence points.

Musical Example 18: Lymburgia, Patrem (BL 122-124)

Musical Example 19: Dufay, Vergene bella (BL 234)

In addition, both cadences are approached by prepared dissonance, which
lasts for the duration of a minim in both Φ and O. Anticipating again,
dissonance of this sort always lasts for one minim in O, C, and C in the
Dufay works, but for a semibreve in ₵, a mensuration in which—contrary to
the practice in Φ—there is a pronounced shift to breve-semibreve movement.
And in certain English pieces in which flagged semiminims indicate augmentation, and movement is in minims and semiminims, dissonance of this sort
lasts for a semiminim. Gafurius, speaking of dissonance in his Practica
musicae, says: "Such dissonance, hidden by syncopation, does not give of-
fense to the ears, however, as this example illustrates:

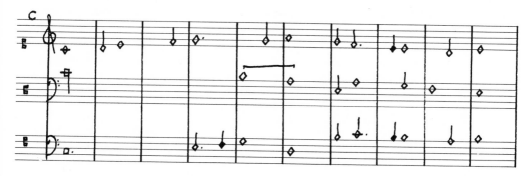

Musical Example 20: Gafurius, Practica musicae III, 4

In this composition, the first minim of the cantus produces a second,
clearly a dissonance, with the tenor. Also the second minim of the cantus
makes a most noticeable dissonance of a fourth with the tenor. In my opinion this should be allowed only rarely, for such a dissonance is noticeable
even when it is found in motion as rapid as one half of a semibreve. Never-
theless, many such as Dunstable, Binchois, Dufay, and Brassart allowed
dissonance of this sort on the minim and semibreve. The next-to-last semibreve of the cantus can be divided into two minims; the first makes a dissonance of a seventh with the next-to-last semibreve of the tenor, but
since the voices are in syncopation, this dissonance is hidden. You will
see the same thing in the next-to-last semibreve of the contratenor when
you divide it into two minims. The first forms a dissonance of a fourth
with the next-to-last semibreve of the tenor, but this is hidden. Minims
or even semibreves making this sort of dissonance must be allowed in counter-
point. In addition to syncopation, there is another kind of hidden dissonance which occurs in compositions, weakening concord. Semibreves in duple
diminution and breves in quadruple, and similarly others, can be retained
even if they make dissonance, since they are equivalent figures to minims."[4]

_____

[4] Gafurius, Practica musicae, 1496, Book III, Chapter IV. ("Atque iccirco
discordantia huismodi sincopata latet nullam auribus afferens lesionem: ut
hoc peipipitur exemplo. ...In hoc concentu: prima minima cantus secundam

The fact that dissonance lasted for a minim in Φ, not a semi-breve, is a strong argument against thinking that this signature called for a duple proportion.

If sections in Φ moved along somewhat faster than O, was the beat in the former a faster beat on the semibreve or a slower beat on the breve? I suggested in the previous chapter that a fast beat on the minim in ₵ was equated with a fast beat on the semibreve in Φ, in pseudo-augmentation. I have also suggested that the function of the cipher 3 at this time was to signal that the two notes which had been falling under the beat, in whatever mensuration it occurred, were to be replaced by three, a usage not dissimilar to the present-day use of the figure 3 to bring about triplets. In O and C, with the beat on the semibreve, a 3 signals that three minims replace two; in Φ, with the beat on the breve, 3 signals for three semibreves to replace two. In the few instances in which a cipher 3 is used in the course of Φ —BL 206, Lymburgia's Tu nephanda prodigi, and Ox 57, Je suy exant by Hugo de Lantins, for example—the effect is the re-placement of two minims by three, not two semibreves by three.

In as late a piece as Josquin's Missa l'homme arme super voces musicales we see from transcription that in the first Kyrie, in which the tenor has ⊙ against a mensuration of O in the other voices, a minim of ⊙ equals a semibreve of O; and in the last Kyrie, in which the tenor has ⊙ against Φ in the other voices, a minim of ⊙ equals a semibreve of Φ. The time-honored idea that two things each equal to a third are equal to one another gives the curious result of O = Φ. The two are identical in organization, and the beat must be on the semibreve in each; the only pos-sible difference between them is that they move at a different tempo.

With the beat on the semibreve in both O and Φ, at a different rate of speed in the two, one would not expect the two mensurations to be used against one another in different voices of the same composition.

---

efficit ad tenorem (patentem quidem discordantiam). Atque secunda pariter minima cantus quarta est ad tenorem notissime discordans: has ego raro con-cederem admittendas: est enim nota ipsarum discordia quanque velociter gradiens dimidium tantum semibrevis obtinet. Complures tamen discordatem huiusmodi minimam atque semibrevem admittebant ut Donstable: Binchoys: & Dufay. atque Brasart. Penultima vero semibrevis cantus in duas minimas distincta: primam minimam cum penultima minimam cum penultima semibrevi tenoris septimam efficit discordem: sed latentem ducente sincopa. Idem quoque comperies in penultima semibrevi contratenoris: quam quum duas in minimas partitus fueris: prima ipsarum ad penultimam tenoris semibrevem quartam discordem monstrabit sed latentem. Qua re minimam huiusmodi atque etiam semibrevem discordantem: in contrapuncto admitti necesse est. Est item & latens discordia in contrapuncto: praeter sincopatam: quae scilicet inter plures cantilenae partes concordes continetur & obtunditur. Semi-brevis autem in duplo diminuta & brevis in quadruplo ac reliquae eiusmodi: que minimae figurae quantitati aequivaleant & si discordantes fuerint in contrapuncto poterunt sustineri.")

Even though Dufay frequently used two different mensurations simultaneously
in pieces written in the 1420's and 1430's, he used O against Φ in only
one piece, the motet <u>Ecclesie militantis</u>—and here in a special way which
will be discussed later.

My suggestion that the beat in Φ was on the semibreve conflicts
with tact-tables of the sixteenth century, which are unanimous in putting
the beat on the imperfect breve in this mensuration, and with the notion of
such present-day scholars as Apel. When Φ was used by sixteenth-century
composers, it was in the way suggested by theorists, with the breve divided
into three semibreves and with two of these semibreves falling under each
tactus, two breves of Φ being sung to three tactus.

Musical Example 21:   16th-century tactus in Φ

But the practice of having the beat on the semibreve in Φ can be
traced in the writings of slightly earlier theorists, of the late fifteenth
and early sixteenth centuries. Adam de Fulda tells us: "O. C. Φ. In these
the semibreve makes the tactus."[5] Ornithoparcus, in his <u>Micrologus</u> of 1516,
says: "Even approved Componists doe erre, because they mark not that there
is a double Progression of measure in a perfect circle divided with a dash,
besides the <u>Ternarie</u> number of the figures, because they are of a perfect
time: singing one <u>Semibreefe</u> to a <u>Tact</u>, when they should sing 2."[6] And as
late as 1535, Ganassi stated flatly in his <u>Opera Intitulata Fontegara</u>, a
work more concerned with practical matters than with theoretical speculation:
"In this signature (₵) the beat must fall on the breve, and in these (O, Φ)
on the semibreve."[7]

There can be little question, then, but that the beat in Φ was on
the semibreve, at least in the first part of the fifteenth century, and that
the line drawn through the circle was not a sign of proportion but merely a
tempo indication. It is even possible to find out what the relationship between the tempi of O and Φ was, bearing in mind that there was no such
thing as a fixed tempo at this time. Ornithoparcus says: "<u>Semiditie</u> is the
middle of the chiefe measure of Notes, which can be placed only in an im-

[5]   Adam de Fulda, De musica. ("O. C. Φ. In his tribus tactum facit semibrevis.")

[6]   Andreas Ornithoparcus, <u>Micrologus</u> (Leipzig, 1516). Translation by John
Dowland (London, 1609), p. 50.

[7]   Silvestro Ganassi, <u>Opera intitulata fontegara</u> (Venice, 1535), chapter 13.
("...de questo signo ₵ richiede la batuda sopra la breve & in questi la
semibreve O Φ.")

perfect time, which hath these Signes, O2. C2. C. ₵. ...Diminution (as
the Ancients thought) is the taking away of the third part from the measure.
But the opinion of the Modernes, is more true and laudable, which makes no
difference betwixt Diminution and Semiditie. ...Therefore Diminution is
the cutting off of the halfe part in the measure, nothing differing from
Semiditie, but that it is found in perfect Signes, and in figures which are
to be measured by the number of 3."[8]

What interests us here is the report that the "Ancients" thought
of diminution as taking away a third, not a half. Coussemaker's Anonymous
XII reports the same practice in the eleventh chapter of his Tractatus de
musica: "When at the beginning a line is found through the middle of a
whole circle not having a dot in the middle, like this: Φ, in this sort of
piece half is not taken away, but only a third part; that is to say, a
third part of the speed it would be sung at if the line were not found
through the middle."[9]

I will offer three musical examples to support the idea that
diminution of a mensuration with triple organization took away a third
part, not a half. The first is an anonymous Et in terra Tr92 147'148,
which begins in C in all voices.

Musical Example 22: anonymous Et in terra (Tr92 147'148)

---

[8] Ornithoparcus, Micrologus, pp. 48-50 of Dowland's translation.

[9] Coussemaker, Scriptorum de musica, III, p. 484. ("Primo quum paragraphum
ponitur in medio unius circuli integri non habentis in medio punctum, et hic:

The tenor changes to Φ; at the same time the two upper voices continue in
the original mensuration but with semibreve coloration, three semibreves of
two minims each replacing two semibreves of two minims each. There is semibreve equivalence between Φ and C with this coloration, making it clear
that in this case the semibreve in Φ has lost a third, not a half, of its
value. Assuming that the beat was on the semibreve in C from the beginning,
it is also on the semibreve in Φ; it must continue to fall on the semibreve
in C with coloration, and the effect of the coloration is to speed up the
beat, to match the faster beat on Φ.

        The second piece, a Pylloys setting of <u>Victime</u> <u>pascale</u> <u>laudes</u>
Tr90 286'287', has a signature of C3 in the superius and contra against ₵
in the tenor, and from a transcription we see that the two mensurations are
equivalent;

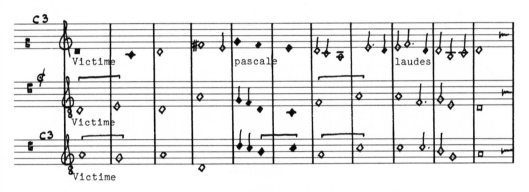

Musical Example 23: Pylloys, <u>Victime</u> <u>pascale</u> <u>laudes</u> (Tr90 286'287)

in each, the breve is divided into two semibreves, the semibreve into three
minims, and there is minim equivalence between the two. In order to under-
stand the function of the line through the signature ₵, calling for diminution, we must go back to the two basic mensurations from which the two signatures in this piece are derived. Assuming minim equivalence between C
and ₵, a semibreve (of two minims) of the former would be two-thirds as
long as a semibreve (of three minims) of ₵. The function of the cipher 3
in C3 is to put three minims in place of the normal two; so a semibreve
(of three minims) of C3 would still be two-thirds as long as a semibreve
(of three minims) of ₵, and there would be neither minim nor semibreve
equivalence between the two. But the line drawn through the signature ₵,
calling for diminution, takes away a third of the value of each minim (and
therefore each semibreve also), resulting in minim and semibreve equivalence
between C3 and ₵.

Φ, hujus modi cantus medietas non tollitur, sed solum tertia pars; hoc
tantum est dicere quod velocius canitur quam (si) paragraphum non
peneretur in medio.")

Belle veullies moy retenir, the third example, is by Dufay himself. The superius has a signature of Φ, the tenor and contra have no
signature but are in tempus perfectum. The piece can be transcribed only
if a semibreve (of three minims) of Φ is assumed to equal a semibreve (of
two minims) of the voices in tempus perfectum. The lower voices must be in
(O), not (Φ), since the latter would give semibreve equivalence between
Φ and Φ, and we have seen that Dufay relates the various mensurations by
minim equivalence at this period. Apparently Dufay thought of a semibreve
(of three minims) of O as being half again as long as a semibreve (of two
minims) of O and used the signal of diminution to take a third away from
the duration of Φ, making a semibreve of this mensuration equivalent to a
semibreve of (O).

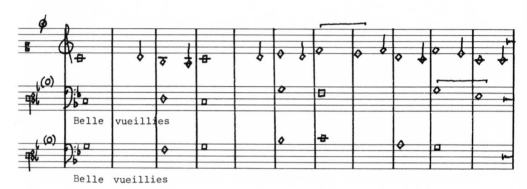

Musical Example 24: Dufay, Belle vueillies moy retenir (Ox 50')

It seems clear, then, that in the Dufay works of this period, Φ
(always organized with three semibreves to the breve),[10] had a beat on the
semibreve approximately half again as fast as the beat on the semibreve in
O. Gafurius equated the normal beat with the human pulse. Assuming a rate
of roughly seventy beats per minute for the pulse, we arrive at a tempo of
approximately seventy semibreves per minute for O (or M.M. = 70, if the
semibreve is transcribed as a quarter note), and slightly over a hundred
semibreves per minute for Φ. It must be remembered that Gafurius was
writing in the 1490's, and the practice he described might have been different fifty years earlier. The important point is the relative speed of the

---

[10] Apel, in his book on notation, assumes that this signature calls for an
organization of three breves per long, with each breve made up of two semibreves. Such a mensuration is called for by the signature O2, but never
in the music of the period or in contemporary writings about this music by
Φ. Sachs also makes the mistake of saying that O2 and Φ call for identical organizations, misreading what "Monk William" has to say about the two.

beats in O and Φ, however, and editors of music from the Dufay era would
be more accurate if they were to use the same scale of reduction for both
O and Φ, and show the difference between the two by a simple tempo indication.

Returning to the question which touched off this discussion, the
matter of the relationship between the similarly organized Φ and ₵3, let
us begin with the assumption that a semibreve of O equals a breve of ₵.
Then two semibreves of ₵ equal one of O, and since the function of the
cipher 3 in the signature ₵3 is to put three semibreves in place of two,
three semibreves of ₵3 equal one of O. If O moves at a rate of approximately seventy semibreves per minute, ₵3 will go at seventy breves or
something over two hundred semibreves per minute, as compared with a speed
of about one hundred semibreves per minute in Φ—bearing in mind, as I
have cautioned before, that the important thing is the relationship of these
figures. Since there is semibreve-minim movement in Φ and breve-semibreve
movement in ₵3, the effect to the ear will be that the section in the
latter mensuration has the same organization as Φ, but moves somewhat
faster. Or it is possible that if the above relationships are observed
quite strictly in a performance, the ear will hear replacement of semibreve-
minim movement (3,2 in this mensuration) by breve-semibreve movement (2,3),
and the effect will be of a change of mensural organization.

The most troublesome piece from this period of Dufay's life, from
the point of view of notation, is the five-voice motet Ecclesie militantis,
which I placed in Group 3 but which raises problems of notation better discussed here. DeVan[11] and Besseler[12] date the piece in 1431, on the assumption that it was written for the coronation of Pope Eugene IV, but Haberl[13]
thought it was written in 1436, when a league was formed by Florence,
Venice and Francesco Sforza against the Visconti, Milan and Genoa. The use
of major prolation in the tenor suggests the earlier date, but the use of
₵ and the presence of colored semiminims points to the latter. It is
printed in the 76th volume of DTO, on pages 26-28, and in the second fascicle of the first volume of the Dufay Opera Omnia, on pages 82-90.

The tenor is built of six colors, each in a different mensuration;
the scheme of the entire piece is:

triplum, motetus: (Φ)	₵		Φ			
contra:		Φ	₵3	Φ		
Tenors:	c	₵	C	₵	O	Φ

[11] G. de Van, Opera Omnia, I (2), p. xxx.

[12] H. Besseler, Bourdon und Fauxbourdon, p. 12.

[13] Fr. X. Haberl, Wilhelm Dufay (Leipzig, 1885), p. 88.

Musical Example 25: Dufay, Ecclesie militantis (Tr87'86)

Musical Example 25: Dufay, Ecclesie militantis (Tr87'86) cont.

The beginning is in pseudo-augmentation. Assuming a beat on the minim in the tenor in C , the beat will fall on the semibreve in Φ in the other voices, since a minim of C equals a semibreve of Φ . The beat must then fall on the imperfect semibreve in ¢ in the second color, with two semibreves (of three minims each) falling under three beats. Assuming a beat on the semibreve in C in the tenor of the third color, the beat will fall on the breve in ¢ and ¢3 on the upper voices and on the breve in ¢ in the fourth color of the tenor.

Thus far, everything fits nicely with suggestions I have made previously about the beat in various mensurations. But assuming a beat on the semibreve in O in the tenor of the fifth color, there would be a beat on the breve in Φ and ¢ in the upper voices and on the breve in Φ in the last color.

Something is wrong, since we began with the beat on the semibreve in Φ and ended with it on the breve in this mensuration. The only set of assumptions which will give the beat on the semibreve in Φ each time it occurs is to have the beat fall on the minim in the tenor for the mensurations C, C, and O and on the imperfect semibreve when each of these is subjected to diminution (¢, ¢, Φ). The difficulty here is that the beat on the minim in C and O is contrary to my findings, as is also the beat on the semibreve in ¢ and ¢3 in the middle section.

Dufay's usual avoidance of simultaneous use of $\mathbb{C}$ and $\mathbb{O}$ (or $\mathbb{C}$), and $\mathbb{O}$ and ϕ, in pieces written after the early 1420's, stems from a re-luctance to bring together two voices with beats of different speeds. None of the complications in <u>Ecclesie militantis</u> are caused by the upper voices, only by the relationship of these voices to the tenor, an artificial voice constructed as a foundation for the piece. The three basic mensurations $\mathbb{C}$, $\mathbb{C}$, and $\mathbb{O}$ are used in the tenor, with minim equivalence assumed among them—although such minim equivalence had given way to other relationships in general mensural practice. Each of the three is subjected to diminution, resulting in a halving of their values—although diminution took a third, not a half, from the value of a triple mensuration in common practice. The upper voices, in diminution throughout, were fitted to this tenor by strict application of the principle that two minims of a mensuration in diminution equal one of a normal mensuration—even though Dufay himself by no means always followed this practice.

Dufay set himself the problem in <u>Ecclesie militantis</u> of using mensurations against one another which would not go together according to performance practice of the time, and he solved this by resorting to theo-retical relationships. It would be a mistake to draw conclusions about mensural practice from this exceptional piece, particularly if they were at variance with conclusions based on an examination of a number of nonexcep-tional works.

Tr87 158'160 is an anonymous motet, <u>Elizabeth Zacharie</u>, with a text drawn from various episodes in the life of John the Baptist. I believe that it was written by Dufay, and that it dates from around 1430.[14] Tr87 is made up of a number of smaller manuscripts brought together in no par-ticular order and bound as a single large manuscript. The motet in question is found in one of the smaller "fascicle-manuscripts,"[15] Tr87 155-166', made up of six double sheets clearly different in content, hand, and type of paper from what comes before and after. The contents are:

Tr87 155-156	Grossin	<u>Patrem</u>
156'157	–	<u>Las aymi quand je pense</u>
157	Ludovicus de Arimo	(textless)
157'158	Dufay	<u>Anima mea</u>
158'160	–	<u>Elizabeth Zacharie</u>
160'161	Ludovicus de Arimo	<u>Salve cara Deo</u>
161'162	Lb	<u>Gentile alma benigna</u>
*162	–	<u>Statuit ei Dominus</u>

---

[14] The piece is published in DTO 76, pp. 16-18.

[15] Cf. C. Hamm, "Manuscript Structure in the Dufay Era," p. 167, for an explanation of this term.

(Tr87)162'164	Georgis a Brugis	Patrem
*164	-	Iste confessor
164'165	Zach. de Teramo	Patrem dominicale
165'166	Jo. Verben	O Domina gloriosa
*166'	Dufay	Festum nunc celebre
*166'	Grossin	Leesse m'amande

* later insertions

Only flagged semiminims are used in pieces which make up the original contents of this fascicle-manuscript; colored semiminims are used in Statuit ei Dominus and Festum nunc celebre, which are among the pieces added at some later date. Concordances are with BL, BU, Ox, Ao, and MuEm. The Grossin Patrem has a mensural scheme of ₵ O ₵, the Brugis Patrem has O₵O₵O₵O₵O₵Φ, the Verben O Domina gloriosa, ΦOΦOΦ. These details indicate that this section of the manuscript contains pieces written before colored semiminims were in use on the Continent and at a time when ₵ and Φ were both in use, probably around 1430.

Six motets attributed to Dufay can be dated between 1426 and 1431: Apostolo glorioso, O gemma lux, Rite maiorem, O sancte Sebastiane, Balsamus et munda, and Ecclesie militantis. Abstracting from them a few, quite general characteristics, we see that Dufay motets of this period were written for four, five, or six voices, and frequently began with a canonic "introitus" for two voices. Only Rite maiorem and Balsamus et munda lack this second feature, in the form in which they have been preserved. These motets used the rare perfect minor mode, in which the long is divided into three breves in the tenor and/or contra. Long rests covering three spaces of the staff, rather than the usual two, are the signal for this unusual mensuration, possible in these motets because the voice or voices in this mensuration always have rests at the start of the motet.[16] They had two colors in the tenor, the first in major prolation (₵ or ⊙) and the second in minor (O, Φ or C). The upper voices sometimes have a series of different mensurations against the first color, but all voices are in the same mensuration for the entire last color. The only exception is Ecclesie militantis, which has six colors—and may not date from this period. But even here, the first colors are in major prolation in the tenor and the last ones in minor, and all voices unite in Φ for the last color.

---

[16] Tinctoris, in De regulari valore notarum, offers a table of signatures in which minor mode is always indicated by the number of spaces covered by a long rest. This tact-table, prescriptive rather than descriptive, is impressively complete and consistent, but it does not answer the question of how minor mode would be indicated in a part which had no long rests.

Elizabeth Zacharie is written for four voices. It begins with a
canonic introitus, for two voices. From rests in the tenor and contra we
see that the long is to be divided into three breves. There are two colors,
the first in major prolation (⊙) and the second in minor (O). The two
upper voices have a string of different mensurations against the first
color, but all four voices join in O for the entire last color. Thus far,
nothing more than a possibility that Dufay could have written the motet has
been established: it is found in a fascicle-manuscript containing other
works of his, and there are general stylistic and structural traits found
in it which can also be observed in Dufay motets of the time.

But even though the four points mentioned above appear to be
quite general, I have been able to find no motet of the period in which all
are observed, except those by Dufay, and Elizabeth Zacharie. Many others
begin with canonic sections for two voices, true enough; BL in particular
contains a large number of such motets by Anthonius Romanus, Ciconia,
Christoforus de Monte, Matheus de Brixia, Fr. Anthonius de Civitato, Grenon,
and Hubertus de Salinas, this list suggesting that the canonic beginning
was cultivated in Italy by both native and visiting composers. But the
other three points cannot be found in any of these. Two motets by Johannes
Brassart come closest. BL 260, a setting of Ave Maria, has the two top
voices in canon at the beginning, rests showing that the long is to be
divided into three breves, and the piece begins in ₵ and ends in O in all
voices. But the canonic beginning is accompanied by the two lower voices,
which always rest for the introitus in the Dufay motets. More important,
the tenor does not have two colors—the piece is not an isorhythmic motet.
BL 279, the Brassart Magne decus, is even more similar to Dufay's practice:
there is a canonic beginning, this time with the lower voices resting; rests
show that the long is perfect; there are two colors in the tenor. But the
entire piece is in O, in all voices.

The upper voices of Elizabeth Zacharie make use of three mensurations (Φ, O and Ɔ) against the ⊙ of the tenor and contra in the first
color, and these are used in just the way Dufay used them at this period.
There is pseudo-augmentation at the beginning, with a minim of ⊙ equal to
a semibreve of Φ. When O is used in the upper voices against ⊙ there is
minim equivalence between the two. Thus Φ and O are both used against ⊙,
but not against one another. Ɔ is introduced in the course of passages in
Φ, but not in O; the effect of the signature is to replace a breve (of
three semibreves) of Φ by a long of two breves (each of two semibreves) of
Ɔ. More simply, four semibreves replace three, just as in the first section of the Missa Sancti Jacobi.

This motet, then, is found in a manuscript which could very well contain a Dufay piece written around 1430, it has certain general characteristics peculiar to the Dufay motets, and it uses several uncommon combinations of mensurations in precisely the way Dufay used them at this time. Thus, I have added <u>Elizabeth Zacharie</u> to my catalogue of the Dufay works, dating it within a few years of 1430.

Distinguishing characteristics: use of ⏀ with flagged semiminims.

*Elizabeth Zacharie
  superius: (⏀) O 2 ⊃ ⏀ O ⏀ ⊃ ⏀ O ⏀ ⊃ O
  motetus: ⏀ O ⏀ ⊃ ⏀ O ⏀ ⊃ ⏀ O ⏀ ⊃ O
  tenor, contra: ⊙   O

O beate Sebastiane
     ⏀

Supremum est mortalibus
   ⏀ ¢3 ⏀

Belle vueillies vostre mercy
     ⏀

C'est bien raison
  (⏀) O ⏀

Vergene bella
  superius: (⏀) O 3 O ⏀
  tenor, contra: (⏀) O   ⏀

* Anonymous, attributed to Dufay by me.

CHAPTER 5
1433-1435

Compositions preserved in manuscripts of the Dufay period are
laid out with superius on the left of an opening, contra or motetus on the
right, and tenor or tenors beneath one or both of these voices. If the
piece requires more than one opening, all voices break off at the same
point (unless the scribe has been careless) and continue on the next opening with the same layout.

A few Dufay pieces are laid out in another way, however. These
are works in which chant and polyphony alternate, sometimes with the indication that the chant is to be sung by "chorus." They are notated with the
voices of each polyphonic section grouped together, alternating with the
chant sections. Where the polyphonic sections require one system or less,
the voices appear to be in score for each section, though the notes are not
lined up under one another accurately. I will use the term "pseudo-score"
for this type of layout.

Dufay works in pseudo-score have common stylistic features: they
are all simple, brief, liturgical pieces; the polyphonic sections are written for three voices, never more nor less; chant is paraphrased in the superius of these polyphonic sections, this paraphrase being so close that it
is little more than transference of the chant melody to mensural notation
with the approach to cadential notes made slightly florid; each piece is
found in one or more of the three manuscripts BL, Tr92 and Tr87; tempus perfectum is used almost to the exclusion of other mensurations; and colored
semiminims are used.

Certain of these pieces are laid out in pseudo-score in one or
more manuscripts but are copied in the more usual way in other sources.
The Trent codices tend to favor pseudo-score, while BL more often has the
normal layout. Notation in pseudo-score is a clue that leads to the bring-
ing together of works sharing many common features; once this has been done,
other pieces can be added to the group—pieces not preserved in pseudo-score
but sharing these common features. Such works are the Kyrie fons bonitatis
and the Et in terra (Tr92 91'92).

Many of the Dufay hymns are notated with the first verse in chant,
the second in three-part polyphony and texts of succeeding verses written
out beneath these first two, alternately. These hymns are found in the same
sections of the same manuscripts that contain the above-mentioned works, and

75

they share the same stylistic features.

Four of the five Magnificats ascribed to Dufay are found in
SPB80, with alternate verses set in three-part polyphony. But this manuscript contains Magnificats by other composers, also arranged in this fashion, which are found in other manuscripts with all verses set polyphoni-
cally.[1] The scribe of SPB80 apparently tailored his Magnificat section to
the performance practice of the church for which he copied the manuscript.
Three of these Dufay Magnificats are found in other sources with all verses
in polyphony, but the Magnificat quinti toni is found in another manuscript,
ModB, with alternate verses, only, in polyphony.

I have brought together as Group 5 all Dufay works notated in one
or more source in pseudo-score, and also those other works sharing the stylistic features of these pieces, excluding those hymns in which: 1) there is
no hint of chant-polyphony alternation; 2) the chant melody is found in a
voice other than the superius; 3) a mensuration other than tempus perfectum
is used.

In the several cases of two settings of the same text in this
style, the two differ as to which lines of text are set in polyphony and
which are left as chant. There are two settings of the untroped Et in
terra:

Tr92 91'92		BL 171
chant	Et in terra	chant
(O)	Hominibus...	-
chant	Laudamus te...	(O)
(O)	Benedicimus te...	chant
chant	Adoramus te...	(O)
(O)	Glorificamus te...	chant
chant	Gratias agimus...	(O)
(O)	Domine Deus...	chant
chant	Domini fili...	(O)
(O)	Domine Deus...	chant
chant	Qui tollis...	(O)
(O)	Qui tollis...	chant
chant	Qui sedes...	(O)
(O)	Quoniam...	chant
chant	Tu solus...	(O)
(O)	Tu solus...	chant
chant	Cum sancto...	(O)
(O)	Amen	chant

---

[1] C. Hamm, "The Manuscript San Pietro B 80," RB, 14 (1960), pp. 44-45.

The two settings of Veni sancte spiritus match up in just the same way:

BL 325^b 326		Tr92 100'101
chant	Veni sancte spiritus...	(O)
(O)	Veni pater...	–
chant	Consolator optime...	(O)
(O)	In labore...	–
chant	O lux beatissima...	(O)
(O)	Sine tuo...	–
chant	Lava quod est...	(O)
(O)	Flecte quod est...	–
chant	Da tuis fidelibus...	(O)
(O)	Da virtutis...	–

At first glance it looks as though Dufay simply made one composition do for two, particularly in the case of Veni sancte spiritus, the Trent version of which does not even offer chant for the alternate verses. But this cannot be the case with the two settings of Et in terra. The superius of the piece in Tr92 paraphrases Mass XI, and that in BL paraphrases Mass XIV; so they cannot be two halves of the same composition.

If it were possible to match up a Dufay piece in this style with an anonymous setting of the same text in which the verses set in polyphony in the piece known to be by Dufay are left in chant in the anonymous work, and vice versa, the chances would be good that the latter piece was also written by Dufay. And this can be done: a Dufay setting of Letabundus exultet (found on both BL 324-325 and Tr92 66'67) matches an anonymous setting of the same text found on Tr92 68'69:

BL (Dufay)		Tr92 (anonymous)
chant	Letabundus exultet...	C
(O)	Regem regus...	–
chant	Angelus consilii...	O
(O)	Sol occasum...	–
chant	Sicut sidus...	C
(O)	Neque sidus...	–
chant	Cedrus alta...	C
(O)	Verbum mens...	–
chant	Isais cecinit...	O
(O)	Si non suis...	–
chant	Infelix propera...	(O)
(O)	Quem docet...	–

Here again it looks as though one composition could have been split up to make two. But though the piece in BL has all of the characteristics of my Group 5, the same is not true of the one in Tr92, which is not

written in pseudo-score, has chant paraphrase in the tenor rather than the
top voice, and has a mensural scheme— CO C CO , with no semiminims in any
of the mensurations—more typical of Dufay works of a decade earlier. The
piece, if it is by Dufay, belongs in Group 1. I have put it there, because
of its relationship to the setting of this text in a piece attributed to
Dufay, because of its proximity to other Dufay pieces of the same type, and
because it resembles the early Dufay works in every way I can determine, in
notational practice and in general style.

        I have put two other anonymous pieces in Group 5, since I believe
they are also by Dufay. The first, a setting of the sequence Mittit ad
virginem, has the scheme:

chant	Mittit ad virginem...
(O)	Fortem expediat...
chant	Naturam superet...
(O)	Superbientium terat...
chant	Foras ejiciat...
(O)	Exi qui mitteris...
chant	Accede nuntia...
(O)	Virgo suscipias...
chant	Audit et suscipit...
(O)	Consiliarium...
chant	Qui nobis tribuat...

        It is found on Tr92 67'68' between the two settings of Letabundus
exultet described above, the first of which is attributed to Dufay. These
three sequence settings could have been copied into this section of Tr92
from the same fascicle-manuscript, and the scribe of Tr92, or of the original fascicle-manuscript, would have intended the attribution to Dufay,
found with the first of the three, to be valid for all of them. The piece
is also found at the very end of BL, on BL 336-337. There are only three
settings of sequence texts in this manuscript, all at the end of the last
fascicle, written in pseudo-score. Two of the three, Letabundus exultet
and Veni sancte spiritus, are by Dufay, and the last one is anonymous. I
attribute it to Dufay because of its close proximity to Dufay pieces in a
similar style in the two manuscripts in which it is preserved, and because
of its stylistic similarity to these pieces.

        The other anonymous piece which I attribute to Dufay, Sancti
spiritus assit, is also a setting of a sequence text. I can find no other
piece in the manuscript in which it is found, Tr92, laid out in pseudo-
score (as this one is) and attributed to a composer other than Dufay. And
it is similar in style and structure to the other sequence settings in
Group 5.

The superius of each of the Kyries in Group 5 paraphrases a
Gregorian Kyrie:

Kyrie Tr92 24	Mass I
Kyrie BL 127	Mass II
Kyrie BL 157^b	Mass IV
Kyrie BL 124^b	Mass IX
Kyrie Tr92 38'	Mass XI
Kyrie Tr92 130	Mass XII
Kyrie Tr87 93	Mass XIV
Kyrie Tr87 94'95	Mass XVIII

The three Glorias in the group paraphrase Mass IX (Et in terra BL 170),
Mass XI (Et in terra Tr92 91'92), and Mass XIV (Et in terra BL 171). Could
Dufay have written these to be paired with certain of the Kyries? Is it
possible that he set out to make settings, in the style of alternate chant
and polyphony, of the various items of certain feasts? For the Feast of
the Ascension we have, in this group, the hymn Jhesu nostra redempcio, the
sequences Rex omnipotens and Victime pascale laudes, and a Kyrie pascale;
the superius of the latter paraphrases the appropriate Gregorian Kyrie, and
the tenor starts off with a quotation from Victime pascali laudes. But the
group cannot be expanded beyond these items. Even though settings of other
parts of this feast (the introit Viri galilei and the Alleluia Ascendit
Deus, for example) are found in manuscripts of the period, none is attributed to Dufay and none of the anonymous settings is in the style of the
pieces of my Group 5. If Dufay did undertake a comprehensive setting of
portions of the liturgy in this style, either he did not get far along with
the project, or much of the music is lost. All that can be done is to pair
sequences and hymns in this style by feasts:

Feast	Hymn	Sequence
Advent	Conditor alme siderum	
Nativity	Criste redemptor	Letabundus exultet
Epiphany	Hostis Herodes	Epiphaniam Domino
Ascension	Jhesu nostra redempcio	Rex omnipotens
		Victime pascali laudes
Pentecost	Veni creator spiritus	Veni sancte spiritus (2)
Holy Trinity	O lux beata	
Corpus Christi	Pange lingua	Lauda syon
Dedication	Urbs beata	
St. Michael	Tibi Cristi splendor	
John the Baptist	Ut queant laxis	
Peter and Paul	Aurea luce	Isti sunt due olive
BVM	Ave maris stella	
All Saints	Criste redemptor	
Apostles	Exultet celum	

A Martyr	Deus tuorum
Several Martyrs	Sanctorum meritis
A Confessor	Iste confessor

Judging from the stylistic unity of the pieces, and from the fact that they are more or less grouped in certain sections of three manuscripts, they probably were all written within a relatively short period of time. Besseler has suggested that this was while Dufay was in Rome as a member of the Papal Choir between the years 1428 and 1433.[2] His reasons for dating these pieces—as well as certain others which do not fall in my Group 5— during this period are that most of them are in tempus perfectum or tempus perfectum diminutum, which he says are typical mensurations of this period of Dufay's work; that some use both ₵ and ∅; and that they are found in one or more of three manuscripts which contain pieces from right around this time. More specifically, he points out that many of them are found in the "Nachtrag" of BL, which contains a newer repertoire than the "Korpus" of this manuscript, and that this Nachtrag must have been copied in 1433 or just a little later. He assumes that Dufay's connection with the Papal Choir prompted him to undertake the composition of a series of brief liturgical pieces.

The latest datable piece in BL is the Dufay motet Supremum est mortalibus, composed in 1433. Besseler places this in his Nachtrag and uses it as evidence that this portion of the manuscript does include pieces dating from Dufay's Roman years. But fascicles 11 and 12, which he considers as part of the Nachtrag and from which he takes a number of pieces for the group of works which he says were written in Rome, were inserted after the original foliation had been put in and, as can be seen from a study of the hand, must date from a somewhat later period than Supremum est mortalibus. We have no terminal date for the pieces in these fascicles or for other pieces clearly added to the manuscript at about the same time. They could date from 1428-1433, but they could also date from five years or more later.[3]

Certainly, many of the pieces which Besseler says were written in Rome between 1428 and 1433 do belong to this period of Dufay's career;

---

[2] H. Besseler, "Dufay in Rom," pp. 1-19.

[3] The difference in semiminim type is a clue that certain compositions and entire fascicles in BL are later than others. The interpolated fascicles 11 and 12 contain eleven pieces with colored semiminims and only two with flagged ones; fascicles 8, 9, and 10, on the other hand, contain eleven pieces with flagged semiminims and only two with colored, and a closer look at the latter two (BL 102, an anonymous Et in terra, and BL 114b, a Dufay Benedicamus Domino) reveals that they are inserted pieces which must be contemporary with those of fascicles 11 and 12.

these can be found in my Group 3 and Group 4. But I believe that the works
which I have grouped in this chapter date from a few years later. Dufay
left the Papal Choir in July of 1433, returning to Italy in 1435. In the
interim he was in Cambrai and Savoy, his appointment to the ducal court of
Savoy taking place during this period. I suggest that the pieces in my
Group 5 were written during the years 1433-1435, when Dufay was in Cambrai
or Savoy, rather than in 1428-1433, when he was in Rome.

I know of no evidence relating the practice of singing liturgical
pieces with alternate verses in chant and polyphony to the Papal Choir at
this time. Nor were composers, known to have been with this group in the
1420's and early 1430's, writing pieces in this style—Dufay being an exception, of course. But there is evidence of this mode of performance in
the North. De Burbure, for example, tells us that in 1431 twenty-one singers were stationed on the left side of Our Lady of Antwerp, and twenty-seven
on the right; by 1443 there were twenty-five singers on the cantoris side
(Ockeghem was among them) and twenty-six on the decani side.[4]

And there is evidence in manuscripts of the period that this type
of setting was practiced by French musicians. Tr87 61-72' is one of the
smaller, self-contained fascicle-manuscripts brought together to make up the
larger manuscript as we know it today. Its contents are:

Tr87 61-63	Dufay	Isti sunt due olive
63'65	Dufay	Epiphaniam Domino
65'67'	Dufay	Rex omnipotens
67'69'	Roullet	Laus tibi Criste
70-71'	Roullet	Sacerdotem Cristi
71'72	Roullet	Omnes sancti seraphim
72'	Roullet	O beata beatorum

All seven pieces are settings of sequence texts, with chant and
polyphony alternating, laid out in pseudo-score. The only information I
have on Roullet is that several other pieces in Tr87 are attributed to him,
as are five in MuEm. He was never listed on the rolls of the Papal Choir,
and from his name he must have been a Frenchman, possibly from the north:
his first name is given as Johannes. It is likely that the seven sequence
settings of Dufay and Roullet had a common origin, since they are so similar in style and layout, and since they are the only pieces contained in
this fascicle-manuscript. There is no reason to suspect that this place of
origin was Rome. The sequences set by Roullet are for the feasts of Mary
Magdalene, Saint Martin, All Saints, and Several Martyrs; there is no duplication of feasts for which Dufay set sequences in this style, and several
of the Roullet sequences are for feasts for which we have Dufay hymns but
no Dufay sequences. It is interesting that the group includes a sequence
from the feast of the patron saint of France.

---

[4] Louis Theunissens, "La musique à Anvers," Annales de l'Académie Royale
d'Archéologie de Belgique, 48 (1906), pp. 173, 189.

Other pieces from this period, all by French composers, are similar in style and/or layout. The Brassart setting of Cibavit eos (Tr92 179')
alternates between chant and three-part polyphony, with chant paraphrase in
the superius of the polyphonic sections, though it is not laid out in
pseudo-score. Tr87 39'43, a Bourgois Et in terra, and Tr92 62'63, a Liebert
Sanctus, are both built of a number of brief sections for three voices; the
superius of the former paraphrase Mass IX, that of the latter Mass IV. The
Bourgois work has the trope Spiritus et alme, set for three voices (pueri,
contra, and tenor), alternating with lines of the Gloria proper. The three
voices of the troped sections are written into the superius part, one under
another in pseudo-score, while the other two voices are written in the
usual place on the opening, with rests for the troped interpolations. The
piece is thus for double chorus, a type of composition which might well
have been an outgrowth of the type of setting with which this chapter is
concerned.

Another reason for suspecting that the pieces in Group 5 were
written after 1433 is the fact that every Dufay piece known to have been
written while he was in Rome for the first time—with the exception of the
troublesome Ecclesie militantis, the date of which is problematic—uses the
older type of flagged semiminim. Among these are two pieces written in
1433, his last year in Rome: C'est bien raison and Supremum est mortalibus.
But every piece in Group 5 uses colored semiminims in every manuscript in
which it has been preserved.[5]

Group 5 gives us a large number of pieces written within a short
span of time from which to draw conclusions about mensural practice. We
see that in the period 1433-1435 the most common mensuration was O, and
that Dufay used Φ and less often, C , for contrast. Major prolation has
disappeared for all practical purposes, and ₵ is not yet in general use,
being found only in two verses of Isti sunt due olive. This latter fact is
most useful, giving us a date (1435) before which pieces using ₵ probably
were not written. Looking back, we see that ₵ is nowhere to be found in
the works of Group 1-4, except in Ecclesie militantis.

In the one instance in which ₵ is used, in Isti sunt, there is a
clear shift from the semibreve-minim movement which prevails in other mensurations to breve-semibreve movement:

---

[5] With the exception of MuEm, a source in which the scribe has not been
concerned with accuracy of detail. Often both types of semiminims appear
in a single composition.

	longs	breves	semibreves	minims	semiminims
verse 16: ¢	2	16	46	15	-
verse 18: O	1	1	16	38	9

Tact-tables agree that the beat was on the breve in ¢. But the eighth verse of Isti sunt has ¢ in the superius against Ф in the contra and tenor. A transcription shows that a semibreve of ¢ equals a semibreve

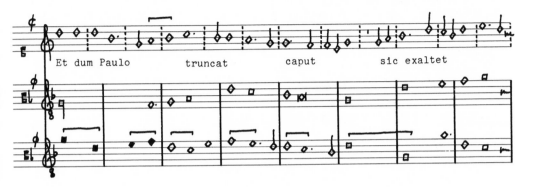

Musical Example 26: Dufay, Isti sunt due olive (Tr87 61')

of Ф; if the beat is on the semibreve in Ф it must also be on the semi-breve in ¢.

There are several possible explanations for this apparent conflict of theory and practice. First of all, the signature ¢ in the upper voice might simply be a mistake for Ф. The superius phrases in groups of three semibreves, like the lower voices in Ф, and every breve in ¢, would be imperfected by the following note or notes if the signature were Ф, i.e., the part would come out just the same in ¢ or Ф. Another possibility is that Dufay disregarded performance practice when writing one mensuration against another in this piece and thought of one minim of any normal mensu-ration as equaling two minims of any diminished mensuration; this is the same suggestion I made for resolving certain difficulties with Ecclesie militantis.

Another solution to this difficulty is to read more closely what theorists have to say about ¢. Ornithoparcus speaks of a "lesser Tact" which "measures by its motion a Semibreefe, diminished in a duple; this is allowed of onely by the unlearned."[6] Martin Agricola explains everything in ¢ in terms of a "halben Tact": a semibreve falls under "ein halben tact," a breve under "2 halben Tact," and so on.[7] The matter is summed up

6 Ornithoparcus, Micrologus, p. 46 of the Dowland translation.
7 Martin Agricola, Musica instrumentalis deudsch (Wittenberg, 1528), p. 43.

quite clearly by Caza, who, after explaining that diminution can be specified by canon and by figures, continues: "Third, diminution can be recog-
nized by a little stroke drawn through the sign of tempus perfectum and
tempus imperfectum. ...This diminution has to do with measure and not with
the form of notes; for such diminution brought about by the use of the
stroke diminishes the measure of the tempus and not the value of the notes.
One can see this clearly in the music itself, for in tempus perfectum the
breve always contains three semibreves and in tempus imperfectum two semibreves in this sort of diminution, just as without it. Diminution effected
by a stroke diminishes the tempus to a half of its original value, as if it
stood in duple proportion. Such diminution is easier than the other types
in reference to execution, division, comprehension and calculation."[8]

The signature ₵, then, signaled that the beat was to shift to
the breve, or that the beat was to remain on the semibreve but to move
along approximately twice as fast as normal. In most pieces of the late
fifteenth and sixteenth centuries in which ₵ is used simultaneously with
some other mensuration, the beat proves to be on the breve. In pieces
which have ₵ in all voices, there is no way of determining from the music
itself which of the two possibilities prevailed in performance. In Isti
sunt the beat must be on the semibreve in ₵, but in most later Dufay works
using this mensuration, the use of sections in (₵)3 suggests a beat on the
breve.

Dufay's equating a semibreve of Ø with a semibreve of ₵ in Isti
sunt is another instance in which a theoretical relationship takes preced-
ence over performance practice in an exceptional piece, the piece in this
case being exceptional because it is the only one in which Dufay uses Ø
against ₵, and the only piece in Group 5 to use ₵ in any way.

Besseler, in "Dufay in Rom," places Isti sunt among the pieces he
believes were written in Rome in the period 1428-1433, because of the use
of both Ø and ₵ in the same piece. But the basic mensuration is O, for
the piece begins in this mensuration and returns to it after each excursion
into another. Ø is used only in the eighth verse. In many Dufay works
written shortly before 1430, ₵ alternates with Ø or is used simultaneously
with it, but there is no such direct contact between the two in Isti sunt.

8
  Francesco Caza, Tractato vulgare de canto figurate (Milan, 1492), p. 20.
("Tertio se cognosce la diminutione per una virgula tracta e traversata per
el signo del tempo perfecto e imperfecto.... E questa proporiamente e
queniente a la mensura del tempo e non a le figure perche per questa diminutione virgulare se minuisse la mensura de esso tempo e non le figure. Il
che se po claramente comprehendre in le compositione cantabile per che nel
tempo perfecto la breve sempre contene in se trey semibreve e nel tempo
imperfecto la breve sempre comprehende doe semibreve cosi in questa diminutione como senza diminutione. Questa virgulare diminutione adonche minuisse
el tempo de meza la sua propria quantita como se fosse in dupla proportione
per che essa diminutione mediale e piu facile in pronunciatione, divisione,
apprehensione e connumeratione de tute le altre.")

Major prolation was seldom used by Dufay after 1430, to be sure, but I believe this is one of the exceptions. The use of colored semiminims and of
¢, both of which indicate that the piece was written after 1433, more than
cancels out the argument that it must date from before 1433 because of the
use of major prolation. I believe that, like the other pieces in this
group, Isti sunt was written for performance in France. Two of the Roullet
sequences found in Tr87 (Laus tibi and Omnes sancti), which are so similar
in style and layout, also have verses in major prolation, and it may be
that this mensuration lingered on longer in France than in Italy, where it
was almost obsolete by this time.

         The fourth verse of Isti sunt, a duo in O, has a passage
in which the cipher 3 is used in both voices, the effect being to replace
two minims by three, just as in earlier works. Minim coloration would have
apparently given the same result, but we can see why Dufay used the cipher
rather than coloration in this passage. Coloration is used in the course
of this section in (O)3; if the passage had been in coloration to begin
with, such a rhythm could have been shown only by using a second color,
something which was done in earlier manuscripts but not at this time.
Dufay achieves the effect of coloration of coloration by using a cipher
and coloration rather than two colors.

         Musical Example 27: Dufay, Isti sunt due olive (Tr87 61)

         The pieces which I have brought together as Group 5 have at-
tracted little attention from scholars, but the fact that so many pieces
can be dated in such a brief period of time gives the group a special
interest.[9]

---

[9] A condensed version of this chapter appeared as "Dating a Group of Dufay
Works," in JAMS, 15 (1962) pp. 65-71.

THE WORKS OF GROUP 5
1433-1435

Distinguishing characteristics: Liturgical pieces notated in pseudo-score; alternation of chant and polyphony; chant paraphrase in superius; colored semiminims

Kyrie pascale Tr92 24
   O ф O

Isti sunt due olive
   O ¢ O C O ¢ O C

Kyrie cum BL 124^b
   (O)

Lauda syon
   (O) ф O

Kyrie de martyribus Tr92 38'
   (O)

Letabundus exultet BL 324-325
   (O)

Kyrie Pater cuncta Tr92 130
   (O)

*Mittit ad virginem
   (O)

Kyrie de apostolis Tr87 93
   (O)

Rex omnipotens
   (O) ф

Kyrie in summis festivitatibus Tr87 94'95
   (O)

*Sancti spiritus assit
   (O)

Kyrie fons bonitatis BL 127
   (O)

Veni sancte spiritus BL 325^{b}326
   (O)

Kyrie cunctipotens genitor BL 157^b
   (O)

Veni sancte spiritus Tr92 100'101
   (O)

Et in terra BL 170
   (O) C O

Victime pascale laudes
   (O)

Et in terra BL 171
   (O)

Magnificat quinti toni
   O C ф

Et in terra Tr92 91'92
   (O)

Aurea luce
   (O)

Epiphaniam Domino
   (O)

Ave maris stella
   (O)

*
  Anonymous, attributed to Dufay by me.

Conditor alme siderum
(O)

Criste redemptor BL 313
(O)

Criste redemptor BL 318[b]
(O)

Deus tuorum
(O)

Exultet celum
(O)

Hostis Herodes
(O)

Iste confessor
(O)

Jhesu nostra redempcio
(O)

O lux beata
(O)

Pange lingua
(O)

Sanctorum meritis
(O)

Tibi Criste splendor
(O)

Urbs beata
(O)

Ut queant laxis
(O)

Veni creator siritus
(O)

I have brought together as Group 6 all works of Dufay which use the mensuration Ø with colored semiminims. Use of this form of the note establishes 1433 as the earliest date any of these pieces could have been written, and there are enough datable works in the group to suggest an approximate terminal date:

1. Salve flos, a motet in praise of Florence and the maidens of the city, must date from 1435-1436. The Papal Court had moved to Florence in 1433; Dufay rejoined the Papal Choir in 1435, remaining with the group in this city through the following year;

2. Nuper rosarum was written for the consecration of the cathedral in Florence on March 25, 1436;

3. Sanctus Papale was probably written while Dufay was with the Papal Choir. Besseler, in "Dufay in Rom," puts this with the works written in Rome during Dufay's first tour of duty with the Choir, but mensural usage has little in common with works known to have been written during the period 1428-1433 and a great deal in common with works written during and shortly after the composer's second period of service with the group. The piece probably dates from 1435-1437;

4. the scribe of Tr92 links the anonymous Agnus custos et pastor with the Dufay Sanctus Papale. Besseler puts it among the Roman works, but it must date from a slightly later time, probably 1435-1437;

5. the "secular motet" Juvenis qui puellam may have been written between 1437 and 1442, while Dufay was doing work at the University of Turin; and

6. the motet Magnanime gentes celebrates a treaty between Bern and Fribourg in 1438.

These dates are clustered between 1435 and 1442. Adding a few years to the last established date, for good measure, I suggest a terminal date of 1445 for the pieces in this group. A surprising implication is that Dufay did not use the mensuration Ø for the last thirty years of his life. This is odd, since other composers used it throughout the century and well into the following one. But no Dufay piece which can be dated after 1445, or which is suspected for one reason or another as having been written after this date, uses Ø. I offer this as empirical data, with no explanation for Dufay's abandonment of it.

In the works of this group, major prolation has disappeared.[1]

---

[1] It is used only in a section of Juvenis qui puellam.

The four basic mensurations are now O, φ, C, and ¢, and a peculiar situation exists among the four. It is clear that φ was thought of as a
diminution (i.e., a lessening but not a halving) of O; in pieces using
both, there is a slight shift of values in the direction of larger notes in
φ, detectable from a count of movement, but scarcely noticeable otherwise.
There is nothing approaching a wholesale shift of values to the next level
of mensuration. For example:

		longs	breves	semibreves	minims	semiminims
Et in terra	O	3	11	60	77	14
Tr92 144'146'	φ	3	9	53	50	10
Agnus Dei						
Tr92 217'218	O	3	7	59	93	17
	φ	2	16	75	70	2
Magnanime gentes	O	1	24	93	114	15
	φ	2	8	50	42	3

Movement is in semibreves and minims in both O   and φ, with
minims outnumbering semibreves in O but semibreves slightly outnumbering
minims in φ. The ratio of breves to minims is higher in φ, and in most
instances a larger percentage of semiminims is found in O than in φ.
These differences in note values are so slight as to be undetectable without a count, however, and the similarity of movement in the two mensurations bears out my suggestion that the difference between the two is one
of tempo.

The situation is not so simple with C   and ¢. To begin with,
it is in the pieces of this group that Dufay first begins to make use of
¢.[2] There is a clear shift from the semibreve-minim movement prevailing
in O to breve-semibreve movement in ¢, suggesting that in this case
"diminution" in the sense of halving takes place:

		longs	breves	semibreves	minims	semiminims
Et in terra	O	3	11	60	77	14
Tr92 144'146'	¢	17	44	63	30	-
Si quereris	O	5	20	97	110	16
	¢	6	26	28	10	-

---

[2] The two earlier pieces using ¢, Isti sunt and Ecclesie militantis,
have already been discussed.

That a relationship approaching a duple proportion is intended
between these two mensurations is verified by the fact that dissonance is
allowed on the minim in O, but on the semibreve in similar figures in ¢.

Musical Example 28: Dufay, Nuper rosarum (Tr92 21'23)

C with semibreve-minim movement is found in only two pieces in
this group, the Et in terra de quaremiaulx and the Sanctus (Tr92 216-217).
Since there is a shift of values between this mensuration and ¢, we are
faced with the perplexing problem of having two mensurations with the same
orgainzation, one written in notes twice as large as the other, apparently
going twice as fast.[3] There would be no difference in the sound of music
written in C and ¢.

There are several possible explanations for this situation.

1. There was not a 1:1 ratio between the speed of the beat on
the semibreve in C and that on the breve in ¢, or a 2:1 ratio between the
beat on the semibreve in C and the semibreve in ¢, but some other ratio,
the difference between C and ¢ being, to the ear, a somewhat different
tempo.

2. It is a chronological matter, pieces using C dating from before those using ¢. No piece by Dufay uses both C and ¢, with the exception of a few isorhythmic pieces which use both in the tenor.

3. Besseler has suggested that ₵ was replaced by Φ because the
new cantabile style of the 1430's made it desirable to have as many ligatures as possible, and Φ made possible many c.o.p. ligatures which would
not have been found in ₵. The same might be true of C and ¢, since more
ligatures are possible in the latter, with its breve-semibreve movement.

There is so little use of C in the pieces of this period that it
is more likely that ¢ replaced C than that the two were different mensurations available to Dufay at the same time.

But the signature C cannot be disposed of so easily. In three
pieces in Group 6 — Fulgens iubar, Magnanime gentes and Si quereris—it is
found before a mensuration moving in breves and semibreves, not semibreves
and minims. A count of Magnanime gentes gives:

---

[3] The Sanctus-Agnus Dei pair (BL 133-134) uses O in the superius and contra
against C in the tenor, a transcription giving the expected result that
there is minim—and semibreve—equivalence between the two.

	maxims	longs	breves	semibreves	minims	semiminims
O	-	1	24	93	114	15
C	1	4	43	51	21	1
¢	-	2	8	50	42	3

On the surface, we have nothing more troublesome here than care-lessness on the part of the scribe, who forgot to draw the stroke through the signature ¢. Two of the three pieces in which this "mistake" is found are in ModB, and there are other examples of the same apparent care-lessness in this manuscript: all sources of the Dufay Supremum est mor-talibus have a signature of ¢3 for the middel section except ModB, which has C3; the Dufay antiphon Hic vir despiciens moves in breves and semi-breves but has a signature of C in ModB; there is exactly the same situ-ation for the antiphons Magi videntes, O gemma martirum, Salve sancte pater, Sapiente filio pater, and the hymn Proles de celo, all attributed to Dufay. All this could be blamed on carelessness, but it is just possible that there is more to this matter.

I have examined Tr87, a manuscript roughly contemporary with ModB and containing Dufay works from the 1420's and 1430's, for varieties of tempus imperfectum.[4] Table I lists pieces using C with semibreve-minim movement, C with breve-semibreve movement, and ¢ with breve-semibreve movement; there are no instances of ¢ with semibreve-minim movement in this manuscript.

TABLE I

TEMPUS IMPERFECTUM IN TR87

Folio	Composition	Type	English Figure
1-2	Et in terra (Dufay)	C(semibreve-minim)	
2'3	Et in terra (Grossin)	C(semibreve-minim)	
3'4	Et in terra (Power)	C(semibreve-minim)	
4'6	Patrem (Power)	C(semibreve-minim)	
6-7	Sanctus (Power)	C(semibreve-minim)	
7'8'	Agnus Dei (Power)	C(semibreve minim)	
9-10	Patrem (anon.)	C(breve-semibreve)	x
12'15	Et in terra (Dufay)	C(semibreve-minim)	
17-18	Sanctus (anon.)	C(breve-semibreve)	
18'20	Agnus Dei (anon.)	C(breve-semibreve)	
20'21'	Sanctus (Bloym)	C(breve-semibreve)	
23-23'	Agnus Dei (Anglicanus)	C(breve-semibreve)	x
25'27	Et in terra (Binchois)	C(semibreve-minim)	
27'29'	Patrem (Binchois)	C(semibreve-minim)	

---

[4] I have excluded the so-called "Battre" section of the manuscript, be-ginning on folio 219, which contains an earlier repertoire and thus has no bearing on the present question.

TABLE I (cont.)

Folio	Composition	Type	English Figure
30'31'	Patrem (anon.)	C(breve-semibreve)	
31'33	Et in terra (anon.)	C(breve-semibreve)	x
33'34	Sanctus (anon.)	C(semibreve-minim)	
34'36	Salve regina (Dunstable)	C(breve-semibreve)	x
		¢(breve-semibreve)	
37'39	Patrem (Power)	¢(breve-semibreve)	
39'43	Et in terra (Bourgois)	C(semibreve-minim)	
		¢(breve-semibreve)	
45'48	Magnificat (Binchois)	C(semibreve-minim)	
58'	Kyrie feriale (Binchois)	¢(breve-semibreve)	
61-63	Isti sunt (Dufay)	¢(breve-semibreve)	
67'69'	Laus tibi (Roullet)	C(semibreve-minim)	
81'82'	Magnificat (anon.)	C(breve-semibreve)	
82'84	Magnificat (anon.)	C(breve-semibreve)	x
88'89	Kyrie (anon.)	C(semibreve-minim)	
95'96	Ecclesie militantis (Dufay)	¢(breve-semibreve)	
97'98	Sanctus (Brassart)	¢(breve-semibreve)	
102'103	Kyrie apostolus (Binchois)	¢(breve-semibreve)	
103'104'	Sanctus (Power-Benet)	C(breve-semibreve)	x
105-105'	Sanctus (anon.)	C(semibreve-minim)	
106'107	Agnus Dei (Power-Benet)	¢(breve-semibreve)	x
107'108	Agnus Dei (anon.)	¢(breve-semibreve)	x
108-108'	Agnus Dei (anon.)	C(breve-semibreve)	x
109'110'	Magnificat (anon.)	C(semibreve-minim)	
115'117	Si quereris (Dufay)	¢(breve-semibreve)	
121'122	Gaude virgo (anon.)	C(breve-semibreve)	x
128	Kyrie (Binchois)	¢(breve-semibreve)	
128'129	Sancta Maria (Dunstable)	¢(breve-semibreve)	x
129'	Kyrie (Binchois)	¢(breve-semibreve)	
130'131	textless (anon.)	C(breve-semibreve)	
138-139	Sanctus (Dunstable)	¢(breve-semibreve)	
139'140	Agnus Dei (anon.)	C(breve-semibreve)	x
141'142'	Et in terra (anon.)	¢(breve-semibreve)	x
144'145	Sancta Maria (anon.)	C(breve-semibreve)	x
145'146	Beata mater (Dunstable)	C(breve-semibreve)	
146'148	Kyrie alma redemptoris (anon.)	C(breve-semibreve)	x
148'149'	Et in terra (anon.)	C(breve-semibreve)	x
150-151'	Et in terra (Binchois)	¢(breve-semibreve)	
151'153'	Patrem (Dufay)	C(semibreve-minim)	
155-156	Patrem (Grossin)	C(semibreve-minim)	
167'174	Mass (Pylois)	C(semibreve-minim)	
		¢(breve-semibreve)	

Nineteen works make use of C with breve-semibreve movement.
Seven of these are attributed to English composers, two others are almost
certainly English (the Kyrie alma redemptoris and the Et in terra alma
redemptoris, Tr87 146'149'), and the others are anonymous. To put it
another way, not a single piece in the manuscript using C with breve-
semibreve movement can be attributed to a non-English composer.

Furthermore, there is reason to believe that five of the ten remaining anonymous pieces using C (breve-semibreve) are also English. In
a previous chapter I called attention to the "English figure," a characteristic melodic turn found in pieces by English composers. A figure of no
more than a few notes may seem slight evidence on which to attribute a composition to a man of a particular nationality, but the more closely the
matter is investigated, the clearer it becomes that this figure was the
almost exclusive property of English composers of a certain era. For instance, I examined all the motets in ModB for this figure and found it in
twenty-eight of them. All twenty-eight are attributed to Englishmen.

Dunstable: Specialis virgo, Salve regina, Virgo mater, Gaude
virgo, Ave regina, Albanus roseo, Sancta Dei, Beata mater, Deus dignus,
Speciosa facta es, Alma redemptoris, Veni sancte spiritus, Gaude virgo,
Sancta Maria, Salve mater, O crux glorioso, Salve schema, Preco preheminen-
cie, Gaude felix, Beata Dei.
Leonel Power: Salve regina, Ibo michi, Salve sancta, Anima mea.
Forest: Tota pulchra, Ave regina.
Polumier: Tota pulchra, Tota pulchra.

I have been able to find this English figure in sixteen pieces in Tr87.
Ten are by English composers, the others are anonymous. (See Table I.)

Both details which are so characteristic of English pieces of
this time—use of C with breve-semibreve movement and use of the English
figure—are found in twelve pieces in Tr87. Five of the twelve are ascribed to English composers, the other seven are anonymous, and I have no
hesitation in suggesting that these latter are English pieces also. They
are:

Tr87	9-10	Patrem
	82'84	Magnificat
	108-108'	Agnus Dei
	121'122	Gaude virgo
	144'145	Sancta Maria
	146'148	Kyrie alma redemptoris
	148'149'	Et in terra alma redemptoris

Adding these to the seven pieces in the manuscript using C
(breve-semibreve) and already known to be English, we have fourteen of the

nineteen works in Tr87 using this mensuration either attributed to English
composers or strongly suspected of having been written by composers of this
nationality. In an earlier chapter I pointed out that OH makes no use
whatsoever of the signatures Φ and ₵, even when these are demanded by the
context. This curious avoidance of an apparently essential indication must
have been characteristic of English manuscripts of this period and shows up
in continental sources with English pieces which must have been copied from
English manuscripts.

The omission of the line through the signature would cause no
difficulty in a performance of the music, however; singers could tell at a
glance whether a piece moved in breves and semibreves, or in semibreves
and minims. If the beat normally fell on the breve in pieces with breve-
semibreve movement, the performer would not need a special signature to
inform him of something which was obvious from the music itself.

English pieces found in continental manuscripts were copied from
English manuscripts, or from other continental manuscripts which had originally been copied from the English ones. We find some English pieces with
the signature ₵ before sections in tempus imperfectum moving in breves and
semibreves, and it may be that the practice among English composers and/or
scribes changed; and there is a chronological difference between English
works using C (breve-semibreve) and those with ₵ (breve-semibreve). It
is more likely, though, that certain continental scribes "corrected" the
signature C when it appeared before a section moving in breves and semibreves; although most scribes were remarkably faithful to their models,
even down to such details as semiminim type and signature, this may have
seemed to be an obvious error to them. A manuscript such as Tr87 may show
an unsystematic mixture of C (breve-semibreve) and ₵ (breve-semibreve) in
English works because parts of it are at least several manuscripts removed
from original English manuscripts, and along the way, some signatures have
been changed from C to ₵ while others have not.

Of the motets found in ModB through folio 102, eighteen have sections in tempus imperfectum with breve-semibreve movement; sixteen have a
signature of ₵, only two have C. From here to the end there are sixteen
motets with tempus imperfectum (breve-semibreve); fourteen have C, only
two have ₵. This suggests that ModB was copied from two or more manuscripts:
those used as models through folio 102 were probably continental, those used
for the remainder were either English or accurate copies of English manuscripts.

Scraps of information found in recent years indicate a closer relationship between Dufay and England than had been suspected. Bukofzer
demonstrated that the tenor of the Dufay Missa caput is a melisma from the
Sarum version of the antiphon Venit ad Petrum,[5] and that there is an English

---

[5] Bukofzer, Studies in Medieval and Renaissance Music, pp. 217-310.

source, in black notation, for a portion of this mass.[6] Even more recently, it has come to light that a sixteenth-century Scottish manuscript, the
"Scone Antiphoner," contains the complete Dufay Missa l'homme arme.[7] Not
only did Dufay know English music, but the English knew his as well. Is it
possible that such Dufay works as the motets Fulgens iubar and Magnanime
gentes which have the English characteristic of the use of the signature
C for sections moving in breves and semibreves owe this peculiarity to the
fact that they were copied into the manuscript which we know them from today from English manuscripts which have disappeared?

        Of particular interest, in view of this possibility, is the group
of four vesper antiphons, attributed to Dufay, copied into ModB in a hand
found nowhere else in the manuscript.[8] They are:

ModB 49'	O gemma martirum	St. George
ModB 50	Salve sancte pater	St. Francis
ModB 50'	Sapiente filio pater	St. Anthony of Padua
ModB 50'	Hic vir despiciens	a confessor not a bishop

        All four, as well as the St. Francis hymn, Proles de celo, copied
in the same hand, have a signature of C, with breve-semibreve movement.
Could this group have been copied from an English manuscript? Is it possible that they have something to do with England? No one has suggested that
Dufay visited England at any time in his life, no evidence of a trip across
the Channel has turned up. It is not my intention to try to make a case
for such a journey on the basis of a handful of pieces showing notational
characteristics usually found in English works; I will merely repeat that
evidence of reciprocal contact between Dufay and England is accumulating.

        Quite aside from these problems brought up by the varieties of
tempus imperfectum, the mere presence of this mensuration in a Dufay work
can be useful in determining the approximate date of composition. Dufay
utilized changes of mensuration for purposes of structure throughout his
life. In early works, he alternated C, O, and C, and tempus imperfectum
in the form of C (semibreve-minim) can be found in works dating as late as
1426, in the motet O gemma lux and in the ordinary sections of the Missa
Sancti Jacobi. Six extended works can be dated between 1427 and 1433—the
proper sections of the latter mass and the motets Rite maiorem, O sancte
Sebastiane, Elizabeth Zacharie, Balsamus et munda, and Supremum est mortalibus—and not one makes use of any variety of tempus imperfectum, contrast

[6] M. Bukofzer, "Caput Redivivum: A New Source for Dufay's Missa Caput,"
JAMS, 4 (1951), pp. 97-110.

[7] Musica Britannica, XV, p. 204.

[8] Except at the end of the hymn section, where Proles de celo, attributed
to Dufay, has been added on 20'21.

coming from alternation of several types of "triple time" (O, Φ, and ¢3).
I date pieces of Group 5 between 1433 and 1435; duple time is found in a
mere handful of these, showing up as C (semibreve-minim) in the <u>Magnificat</u>
<u>quinti toni</u> and the <u>Et in terra spiritus et alme</u> and as ¢ in <u>Isti sunt</u>.
Dufay almost abandoned tempus imperfectum for the period 1427–1435. But beginning with the motets <u>Salve flos</u> (1435-1436) and <u>Nuper rosarum</u> (1436) and
continuing right up to the end of his life, Dufay used ¢ (breve-semibreve)
in every mass and motet, and in many shorter pieces as well.[9] The most
common mensuration patterns in these later works are O ¢ O and such variations as O ¢ Φ and O ¢ O ¢ O, as can be seen from a glance at the lists
of mensurations in Groups 6-9.

Fifty-two motets in ModB are ascribed to English composers.
Forty-one of these make use of some sort of tempus imperfectum; most of the
remaining eleven are brief works in a single section, written in tempus
imperfectum throughout, examples being the Leonel Power settings of <u>Salve</u>
<u>sancta parens</u> and <u>Mater ora</u>. Even more significant, well over half of these
English motets are constructed with the O ¢ O pattern so prevalent in the
later Dufay works. These are:

Dunstable: <u>Virgo mater</u>, <u>Gaude virgo</u>, <u>Ave regina</u>, <u>Albanus roseo</u>,
<u>Sancta Dei</u>, <u>Salve regina</u>, <u>Deus dignus</u>, <u>Christe sanctorum</u>, <u>Alma redemptoris</u>,
<u>Veni sancte spiritus</u>, <u>Gloria sanctorum</u>, <u>Gaude virgo</u>, <u>O crux glorioso</u>, <u>Salve</u>
<u>scema</u>, <u>Preco preheminencie</u>, <u>Gaude felix</u>, <u>Beata Dei</u>.
Leonel Power: <u>Salve regina</u>, <u>Anima mea</u>.
Polumier: <u>Tota pulchra es</u>.
Benet: <u>Telus purpuri</u>, <u>Lux fulget</u>.
Forest: <u>Gaude martir</u>.
Sandley: <u>Virgo prefulgens</u>.

Certainly continental composers of the generation of Dufay were
strongly influenced by the music of their contemporaries in England. There
is literary evidence of this, the most widely quoted document being Martin
le Franc's "Le Champion des Dames," one verse of which says:

For they (Binchois and Dufay) have adopted a new practice
Of making pleasing concordance
In high and low music,
In feigning, in rests, and in mutation,
And have assumed the English countenance,
And follow Dunstable,

---

[9] The few exceptions will be noted as they come up.

To make their joyful and distinguished music
Wonderfully pleasant.[10]

Tinctoris reported the same situation in the preface to his
Proportionale musices: "At this time, consequently, the possibilities of
our music have been so marvelously increased that there appears to be a
new art, if I may so call it, whose fount and origin is held to be among
the English, of whom Dunstable stood forth as chief. Contemporary with
him in France were Dufay and Binchois."[11]

There has been much speculation as to the precise time of Dufay's
contact with English music and as to just what changes this contact brought
about in his own music. Besseler, in Bourdon und Fauxbourdon, suggests
that the contact was in Paris around 1427, and that faulxbourdon was an off-
spring of this intercourse. Bukofzer says that Dufay adopted the English
"pan-consonant" style, without contrasting specific examples of pre-pan-
consonant Dufay with others of post-pan-consonant Dufay.[12]

I have discussed certain changes in notational practice which can
be observed in Dufay works written in 1433 and shortly thereafter. Summa-
rizing these:

1. Dufay used flagged semiminims prior to 1433, colored ones
after this. I can find no music by other continental composers written
before 1433 with colored simiminims, but twenty-one of the twenty-four
pieces with semiminims in OH—which is now thought to date from well before
1433—use the colored type. This must have originated in England, and Dufay's wholesale incorporation of it into works written after 1433 might be
a clue that he had come into contact with English music at just this time.

2. Dufay made sparing use of tempus imperfectum during the period
1427-1435 but extensive use of it after this. More specifically, he used a
mensuration moving in semibreves and minims under the signature C before
1427, and after 1435 he used breve-semibreve movement under the signature
₵, or sometimes C. The latter mensuration is common in English music before 1433, examples being the Damett Et in terra (OH 9'10), the Excetre
Et in terra (OH 15'16), the Cooke Et in terra (OH 32'33), the Sturgeon Et
in terra (OH 34'35), and many other pieces in this and other manuscripts.

---

[10] Stainer, Dufay and his Contemporaries, p. 13.

("Car il (z)ont nouvelle pratique
De faire frisque concordance
En haulte et en basse musique,
En fainte, en pause et en muance,
Et ont pris de la contenance
Angloise, et ensuivy Dunstable,
Pourquoy merveilleuse plaissance
Rent leur chant joyeulx et notable.")

[11] Translation from Oliver Strunk, Source Readings in Music History (New
York, 1950), p. 195.

[12] Bukofzer, Studies in Medieval and Renaissance Music, p. 257.

3. Dufay obtained contrast between sections of extended compositions written before 1427 by alternation of ℂ, O, and C. Between 1427 and 1435 he used O, Φ, and ₵3 for contrast. After 1435 he used O and ₵, and sometimes Φ, the most common pattern begin O ₵ O, or some variation on this. This pattern is characteristic of English music of this time.

These are superficial details of mensural practice which have nothing to do with the sound of the music, or its structure. But the basic idea underlying this book is that such superficial details can give important clues as to who might have written a certain piece, when the piece was written, and what other works influenced a particular composition or were influenced by it. Details of notation tell us nothing about the music itself, but they may suggest starting points for further studies of this music.

Another stanza of "Le Champion des Dames" follows:

You have heard the English
Play at the Burgundian court.

. . . . .

I have seen Binchois in shame,
Silent, listening to their rebecs,
And Dufay, angry and frowning
Because his own melodies are not so beautiful.[13]

Dufay and Binchois at the Burgundian court, hearing English musicians perform their own works to the discomfort of the two Frenchmen! This is significant information, particularly if it is possible to determine when the incident took place. Stainer points out that the fourth book of this poem, in which the passage is found, must date from between 1436 and 1444.[14] We know little about the actual contact between Dufay and Binchois, but the music of the two developed in such similar ways that such contact must have been frequent. There is an almost complete lack of datable pieces by Binchois—the motet Nove cantum melodie of 1430 is the only one, to my knowledge—but exactly the same stages of notational practice that I have found in the music of Dufay can be traced in Binchois, and these changes must have taken place at the same time in the music of the two men.[15]

---

[13] Stainer, Dufay and his Contemporaries, p. 13.

      ("Tu as bien les Anglois ouy
      Jouer a la cour de Bourgongne.
              . . . . .
      J'ay veu Binchois avoir vergogne
      Et soy taire empres leurs rebelles,
      Et du Fay despite et frongne
      Qu'il n'a melodie si belle.")

[14] Ibid., p. 12.

[15] Cf. Robert Marshall, "The Mensural Practice of Gilles Binchois," Princeton (unpublished seminar report), 1961, for confirmation of this statement.

We know that Dufay was in France between 1433 and 1435, and I
have pointed out notational changes in his music which took place at just
this time. The same changes can be observed in the music of Binchois at
what I assume to be the same time. These changes are of a nature which
brought the music of the two continental composers more in line with English practice.

Therefore, I suggest that between Dufay's two periods of service
with the Papal Choir he came into contact with English music written by
such men as Leonel Power and Dunstable. This contact took place at the
Burgundian court, sometime between 1433 and 1435, and Binchois shared in
this contact. English music influenced Dufay's own music in ways which can
be detected at the superficial level of notational practice, and it must be
detectable in other aspects of the music. A stylistic analysis of Dufay's
works undertaken to determine the influence of English music would do well
to concentrate on the works of the early 1430's.

Dufay was an experienced and even famous composer by this time.
Why not assume, if there are similarities between his music and that of
English composers, that the latter learned from him? For one thing, literary evidence emphasizes that " new" features were found in English music.
For another, English works which must date from before 1433 contain notational features found in Dufay's music only after this date. One such
piece is the Patrem (BL 111), attributed to "de Anglia," which has the pattern O C φ, with breve-semibreve movement in C; it is similar in every
obvious way to English pieces in such manuscripts as ModB, but from its
location in BL it can be assumed to date from before 1433. Similar works
are the Excetre Et in terra (OH 15'16) and the Sturgeon Et in terra (OH
34'35).

Several minor points of notational interest come up in the pieces
of Group 6. The sign $\frac{6}{4}$, found in the course of a section in C(semibreve-
minim) in the Sanctus (Tr92 216-217), is the only example I have found in
the works of Dufay of a fraction, a signature with both a numerator and a
denominator. Organization under this unusual signature is the same as that
of tempus perfectum—the breve has three semibreves, each of two minims—
but the two mensurations are not equivalent. Assuming minim and semibreve
equivalence between O and C, a breve of O would be half again as long as
one of C, since it is made up of three semibreves as opposed to two in C.
But in this case a breve (of two semibreves) of C is equal to a breve (of
three semibreves) of (C)$\frac{6}{4}$; so each semibreve and minim of the latter has
a value of only two-thirds that of each semibreve and minim of the former.
The function of the signature $\frac{6}{4}$, then, is to substitute another relationship for the usual minim equivalence between O and C. Six minims of the
new mensuration replace four of the original; as is always the case with
Dufay, the signature has to do with relationships at the minim level. A
signature of (C)$\frac{3}{2}$ would have indicated the same relationship but might

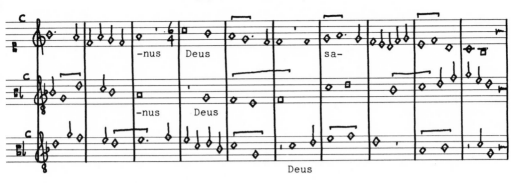

Musical Example 29: Dufay, Sanctus (Tr92 216)

have implied to the performer that minims were to be grouped in two units
of threes rather than three units of twos.

The cipher 3 is used exactly as it was in Dufay's earlier works:
when it occurs in the course of O, it signals that three minims are to replace two; when found in ¢, it calls for three semibreves to replace two.
Both usages can be seen in the Agnus custos et pastor. In Magnanime gentis
and Si quereris the cipher 3 occurring in sections of C calls for three
semibreves to replace two, not three minims to replace two as might have
been expected. But in both pieces C has breve-semibreve movement and is
equivalent to ¢, as this use of the cipher 3 verifies.

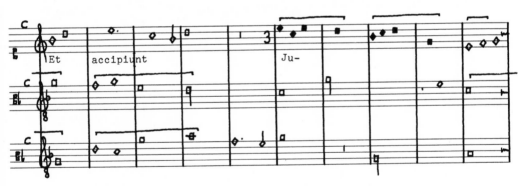

Musical Example 30: Dufay, Si quereris (Tr87 116'117)

The cipher 3 in the course of ¢ is followed by the cipher 4 in
the last section of Salve flos. The effect is cumulative: the 3 indicates
that three semibreves are to replace two, the 4 that four semibreves are to
replace three of (¢)3. Coloration in (¢)4 has the effect of replacing
two normal breves by three colored ones.

The pieces of Group 5 were characterized by chant-polyphony alternation and close paraphrase of chant in the superius part of the polyphonic

Musical Example 31: Dufay, Salve flos (ModB 64'65)

sections; both characteristics can be found, in modified and more complex
form, in certain pieces in Group 6. The Sanctus (Tr92 216-217), for example, has a superius based on the appropriate chant from Mass VIII, but
the paraphrasing is done with much more freedom than was the case in the
simpler pieces of Group 5. And a more flexible structure replaces rigid
alternation of chant and polyphony:

                    Sanctus   chant ("chorus")
                    Sanctus   two-voice polyphony
                    Sanctus   three-voice polyphony
                    Pleni sunt   two-voice polyphony

Osanna	three-voice polyphony
Benedictus	chant ("chorus")
Qui venit	two-voice polyphony, plus faulxbourdon
Osanna	three-voice polyphony

Tinctoris, in the third chapter of the first book of his _Proportionale musices_, reports that Dufay used the signature O3 to indicate a "duple sesquiquarta" proportion in the "Qui cum patre" section of his _Missa Sancti Antonio_.[16] Later in the same chapter he quotes a section of the _Et in terra_ from the same mass as a demonstration of the "correct" simultaneous usage of C and O, his point being that there should be minim equivalence between the two.[17]

Tr90 72'73 is a _Kyrie_ ascribed to Dufay, at the end of which some-one has scribbled in the manuscript "Et in terra et totum officium quaere post missam Badingm." Tr90 383'385' is an _Et in terra_ ascribed to "Bedingham Langensteiss" built over a tenor labeled "Deul angouisseux," which Ficker claims is based on the Binchois ballade of this name;[18] a _Patrem_ (Tr90 386'389), a _Sanctus_ (Tr90 389'392) and an _Agnus Dei_ (Tr90 392'395) follow, and the editors of the thematic index of the Trent codices have labeled the tenor of each of these "Deul angouisseux," under the assumption that the four consecutive sections form a mass without a Kyrie. Immediately following are an anonymous _Et in terra_ (Tr90 395'398), _Patrem_ (Tr90 399' 403), _Sanctus_ (Tr90 403'405) and _Agnus Dei_ (Tr90 405'406); these sections seem to be the ones to which reference is made in the note after the Dufay _Kyrie_. The "Qui cum patre" section does use the signature O3, C is used against O with minim equivalence between the two in the _Et in terra_, and this passage agrees with the one quoted by Tinctoris. It appears as though these four sections, together with the _Kyrie_, make up the Dufay _Missa Sancti Anthonii_.

Dufay's will mentions two Saint Anthony masses, the _Missa Sancti Anthonii de Padua_ and the _Missa Sancti Anthonii Viennensis_. Besseler iden-tifies the mass found in Tr90 with the latter: "Giovanni Spataro, in an unpublished letter of about 1532 to Pietro Aron, cites several examples from the Gloria of Dufay's _Missa de Sancto Antonio de Padoa_. Since none of these citations appears in the Gloria Trent no. 1102, we may conclude that the mass for three voices of the codex Trent 90 is Dufay's _Missa Sancti Anthonii Viennensis_. This mass, the very early work _Missa sine nomine_, and the somewhat riper _Missa Sancti Jacobi_ form together the first group of mass cycles."[19]

---

[16] Tinctoris, _Proportionale musices_, printed in Coussemaker, Scriptorum, IV, p. 156.

[17] Ibid., p. 171.

[18] R. Ficker, "Die frühen Messenkompositionen der Trienter Codices," SzMW, 11 (1924), pp. 56-57.

[19] H. Besseler (ed.), _Guglielmi Dufay: Opera Omnia_, III, p. 1.

If these five sections do indeed form one mass, and if this mass is by Dufay, it belongs with the works of Group 6 and can therefore be dated between 1433 and 1445, since it makes use of the signature Φ and has colored semiminims. Besseler accepts it as a Dufay work, finds that it fits nicely into the development of his treatment of the mass, and prints it in one of the mass volumes of the <u>Opera Omnia</u>.[20]

Despite this impressive evidence in favor of Dufay's anthorship, some scholars have been reluctant to accept the mass as authentic. De Van, for example, in the introduction to the third fascicle of the <u>Opera Omnia</u>, says that he cannot accept the authenticity of even the Kyrie, on stylistic grounds. Unfortunately, he does not explain just what there is about the piece which makes him question Dufay's authorship.

But there are many clues that something is wrong with the whole business. To begin with, the four mass sections found on Tr90 383'395 do <u>not</u> form a mass by Bedingham. The <u>Gloria</u> and <u>Credo</u> belong together: they are built on the same tenor; the upper two voices begin in similar fashion; and the two are grouped in another manuscript, the <u>Gloria</u> being found on Tr88 27'29 and the <u>Credo</u> immediately following, on Tr88 29'30'. The <u>Sanctus</u> and <u>Agnus</u> which follow in Tr90, however, have nothing to do with the two preceding sections, being built on a different tenor and having no relationship whatsoever to the <u>Gloria</u> and <u>Credo</u>. Such composite masses are common in this manuscript. In this case it is possible to locate the <u>Sanctus</u> and <u>Agnus</u> which complete the Bedingham <u>Missa deul angouisseux</u>: the <u>Sanctus</u> is found on Tr88 17'19' and the <u>Agnus</u> just after it. The initial identification of these sections is simplified by their use of the unusual signature C 2, with which the first two sections of the Bedingham mass also begin; when it is seen that all four sections are built over the same tenor and have similar beginnings in the upper voices and the same pattern of clefs and key signatures, we can bring together the following as the Bedingham <u>Missa deul angouisseux</u>:

<u>Et in terra</u>	Tr88 27'29; Tr90 383'385'
<u>Patrem</u>	Tr88 29'30'; Tr90 386'389
<u>Sanctus</u>	Tr88 17'19
<u>Agnus Dei</u>	Tr88 19'21

The pattern of clefs and key signatures of the four sections which the editors of the Trent thematic catalogue thought made up the Bedingham mass should have suggested that the four did not go together:

<u>Et in terra</u>	soprano	alto[b]	alto[b]
<u>Patrem</u>	mezzo	alto[b]	tenor
<u>Sanctus</u>	soprano	tenor	tenor
<u>Agnus Dei</u>	soprano	tenor	tenor

---

[20] <u>Ibid.</u>, II, pp. 47-68.

A similarly confused situation exists with the clefs and key signatures of the "Missa Sancti Anthonii":

Kyrie	soprano	tenor	tenor
Et in terra	mezzo	tenor(b)	tenor(b)
Patrem	soprano	alto(b)	alto(b)
Sanctus	soprano	alto(b)	alto(b)
Agnus Dei	soprano	alto(b)	alto(b)

The superius part of the last Kyrie is written a third too high
in Tr90. A possible explanation for this mistake is that the scribe was
copying from a model which had this voice in the mezzo clef, and simply forgot to indicate the proper clef here. If this were the case, we could assume that the Kyrie and Gloria had originally been paired by clefs, and
that the last three sections are another group with a different set of clefs.
There is some justification in the music itself for such a division; the
Kyrie and Et in terra have certain motifs in common, as do the last three
sections, while there is no apparent thematic relationship between the
first pair and the last three. Only the Et in terra can be identified from
the Tinctoris treatise, after all. Is it possible that the Kyrie and the
Et in terra are by Dufay, and that these have been brought together in this
manuscript with a Patrem, Sanctus, and Agnus Dei by another composer? There
is, immediately preceding, an example of groups of mass sections from two
different works brought together by the scribe of Tr90 as a composite mass.

The basic assumption of this book is that Dufay was consistent in
his use of signatures and mensurations and other details of mensural practice in any given period of his life, and that this practice changed from
period to period. As I have already pointed out, if this mass is by Dufay
it belongs in Group 6 because of its use of Φ with colored semiminims.
Also, the Kyrie and Agnus Dei have the O¢O pattern so common in works of
this group, as do the Et in terra and Patrem, though the pattern is much
elaborated in the latter two. But in this mass, as it is preserved in Tr90,
there are six details of mensural practice which conflict with Dufay's practice of this period as it can be reconstructed from other works.

1. The signature $\frac{O}{3}$, used in the Et in terra, is found in no other
Dufay work. The function of the signature is clear enough, since it is
found in only one voice against Φ in the other two voices: transcription
shows that a breve of three semibreves in $\frac{O}{3}$ is equivalent to a breve of
two semibreves of Φ. Separated coloration occurs under this signature;
both the breve and semibreve lose a third of their value, and the passage
is so ambiguous in rhythm that it is not clear whether this should be con-
sidered breve or semibreve coloration. (See Musical Example 32.)
The signature $\frac{O}{3}$ is found in works of such later composers as Josquin, Domarto, Vaqueras, Brumel, Busnois, and Compere, but not in other
works by Dufay, from this period or later. It has exactly the same effect

as the signature ₵3, which is used later in this very section of the mass, and at no time have we seen Dufay using two different signatures to bring about identical results.

Musical Example 32: <u>Missa</u> <u>Sancti</u> <u>Anthonii</u>, "Domine Deus" (Tr90 396'397)

    2. The section quoted by Tinctoris, in which ₵ is used against O, has flagged semiminims in the voice in ₵ and colored ones in the voice in O.

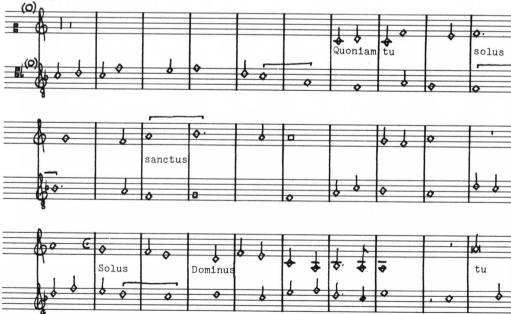

Musical Example 33: <u>Missa Sancti Anthonii</u>, "Quoniam tu solus" (Tr90 397'398)

Dufay used flagged semiminims in all mensurations in works written before
1433 and colored ones in all mensurations in works written after this.
There is no other work in which he uses both in the same piece.

      3. In this same section of the <u>Et in terra</u>, the signature Ɔ is
introduced in the superius in the course of the mensuration ₵. The effect
is the same as in the early Dufay works in which this signature is used:
a breve (of four minims) replaces a semibreve (of three minims). The lower
voice continues in O throughout this section, the relationship between it
and Ɔ being that two breves of two semibreves each (the semibreve having
two minims) of Ɔ are sung in the time of one breve of three semibreves
(each of two minims) of O. Thus there is a 4:3 ratio at the minim level
between Ɔ and O (see Ex. 33). The cipher 3 is introduced at the end of the
section in the superius, replacing two minims of Ɔ by three of (Ɔ)3. In
relation to the other voice, six minims of (Ɔ)3 are equivalent to three

minims of tempus perfectum, but the relationship is more complex than this
description suggests: twelve minims of (Ɔ)3, grouped as 4 × 3, sound in
the time of six minims of O, grouped 3 × 2, with a <u>Grosstakt</u> of a breve
between the two mensurations.

There is no other example of Dufay's using Ɔ against O, nor of
his use of (Ɔ)3.

4. The "Crucifixus" section of the <u>Patrem</u>, which has ₵ in all
three voices at the beginning, ends with a section in Ɔ in the superius.

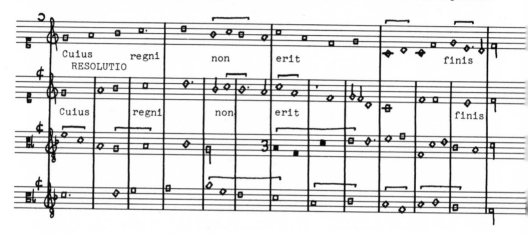

Musical Example 34: <u>Missa Sancti Anthonii</u>, "Crucifixus" (Tr90 400'401)

Dufay, in his other works, used the latter signature only in relation to ₡
or ₵. In the present piece, its function is to place four breves of two
semibreves (each of two minims) in the space taken up by three breves of
two semibreves (of two minims) of ₵. This relationship would cause some
difficulty in performance: if the beat were on the breve in ₵, the singer
of the superius part would have to sing four breves against three beats,
and if the beat were on the semibreve in ₵ he would have to sing four
breves (or eight semibreves) against six beats. Tr90 gives an alternate
version of this passage, a "resolutio" reducing it to the same mensuration
as the other parts, simplifying the line somewhat in the process.

5. In the "Et in spiritum," in the course of a duet in ₵, the
signature O3 is introduced in the superius. This must be the passage described by Tinctoris: "In this Dufay in his 'Qui cum patre' from the Mass,
'Sancto Anthonia,' has most wonderfully erred, for there he has desired to
signify that very proportion, i.e., duple sesquiquarta, since he has referred 3 perfect breves to 2 imperfect ones. ...In this indeed he ought to
have signified it thusly: O_4^9; for it is not sesquialtera, nay rather, as
we have shown above, as is obvious, it is duple sesquiquarta."[21]

---

21 Tinctoris, <u>Proportionale musices</u>, Seay translation, p. 45.

The effect here is that a long of two breves (each of two semi-breves) of ₵ is equivalent to a long of three breves (each of three semi-breves) of O3.

Musical Example 35: <u>Missa</u> <u>Sancti</u> <u>Anthonii</u> (Tr90 401'402)

Since a long of ₵ equals a long of O3, there is no proportion between the two mensurations at this level; at the breve level there is a 3:2 relation-ship, or a sesquialtera proportion; there is a 9:4 relationship, or a duple sesquiquarta proportion, at the semibreve and minim levels, as Tinctoris points out. The intent of the composer was to show that three breves of O3 were to replace two breves of ₵, and the cipher 3 is used here to show a 3:2 relationship, as usual. But we have seen that Dufay indicated relation-ships between mensurations only at the minim level, or at the semibreve level in those diminished by half—never at the breve level.

Dufay often uses the cipher 3 in the course of O to indicate that three minims were to replace two. Is this the same as the use of O3 as a signature? If so, we see still another departure from his normal men-sural practice in this piece, since he would not use the same signature to mean two quite different things. And there is every reason to believe that if Dufay had used O3 as a signature, its meaning would have been the same as (O)3. He used the cipher 3 in ₵ to indicate that three semibreves were to replace two; and whenever he used ₵3 as an initial signature, in <u>Supre-mum</u> <u>est</u> <u>mortalibus</u> for example, the resulting mensuration was just the same. (₵)3 was identical with ₵3. O3 and C3 are seldom used as initial signa-tures at this time, but when they do occur, they invariably call for a men-suration in which the 3 has put three minims to the semibreve. An example is the anonymous three-voice setting of <u>L'homme</u> <u>arme</u> in Mel, with a signa-ture of C3 in all voices.

6. All voices in the "Et unam sanctam" section of the Patrem move along in O until the "Amen," where the superius has ₵ against con-tinuation of O in the contra and tenor. The composer has thought of O and ₵ as being in a 2:1 ratio, with a minim of O equaling a semibreve of ₵. Dufay avoided using these two against one another, since in his normal practice there was no simple ratio between them. (See Ex. 36.)

There is a danger, in a study such as this, of extracting rules from usual practice and insisting that these were invariably followed.

Musical Example 36: Missa Sancti Anthonii (Tr90 402'402)

Every composer has the privilege of experimenting and of changing details
of his style, and there are pieces by Dufay with unique features of notational practice. But when departures from normal practice are as numerous
as in this piece, serious doubt must be cast on its authenticity.

        Another factor must be considered in this case, however. I have
assumed throughout this study that the Dufay works have been preserved in
the various manuscripts in essentially their original form, and that details
of notational practice can be taken to be what Dufay himself intended. I
have shown that in most manuscripts, scribes took care to duplicate even
minute details of the pieces they were copying. But Tr90, the manuscript
containing the Missa Sancti Anthonii, is exceptional in that it abounds in
mistakes and deviations of many sorts.

Musical Example 37: Binchois, Asperges me (BL version)

Example 37, a comparison of the beginning of the Binchois <u>Asperges</u> <u>me</u> as it is found in BL and Tr90, illustrates the most common type of deviation found in the latter source. The superius and tenor parts are essentially the same in the two manuscripts, but the contra uses a different clef in Tr90, and there is considerable variation in ligatures and even in actual notes. This might be taken as an example of the unreliability of BL, rather than Tr90, were it not for the fact that the latter so consistently disagrees with other manuscripts.

Musical Example 38: Bedingham, <u>Et in terra</u> (Tr88 28'29)

Example 38 is a portion of the Bedingham <u>Et in terra</u> (Tr90 385'). The superius, which has been in tempus perfectum to this point, has a passage in ◯, and from a transcription, we see that this signature is used here to bring about a quite different situation from what we normally find: four colored semibreves of ◯ replace one of O, or six colored breves of ◯ replace one normal breve of O. The same piece is found on Tr88 28'29, and in this source the superius continues in O to the end of the section, with no change of signature and no coloration. The obvious assumption would be that the version in Tr90 must be closer to the original, since it seems more likely that the scribe of Tr88 would have simplified a difficult passage than that the scribe of Tr90 would have introduced mensural complications not found in his model.

But Feininger reports another case in which the scribe of Tr90 appears to have tampered with a piece he was copying, the composition in this case being the <u>Alleluia</u> <u>veni</u> <u>sancte</u> <u>spiritus</u> found in both Tr88 (anonymous) and Tr90 (attributed to Dufay): "In the version of Trento 90 the last five measures of the Alleluia are different, and in the Versus the measures 83-100 are simply left out: the connection of the two remaining parts has been re-established by some act of composition. The text is the same, and the original melody therefore is also the same. It can hardly be presumed that we have two different original versions by the author himself. In all other compositions, those which are known under his name as well as those which have been attributed to him by us, Dufay scrupulously follows the exact course of the Gregorian melody in its every single note, adding to its length through floscules of his own rather than shortening it in any way. It seems obvious that somebody has been tampering with this composition. There is no plausible reason why Dufay should have, in the first instance, shortened the piece by that melisma which in Trento 90 is missing, and that either he himself, or somebody after him should have later, in a second instance, added the missing part."[22]

I have already pointed out that the four sections of the Bedingham <u>Missa</u> <u>deul</u> <u>angouisseux</u> as found in Tr88 have the same clefs and key signatures, while the two sections of the mass found in Tr90 do not agree with Tr88, or even between themselves, on these matters. There is a further difference between the two versions of the <u>Patrem</u>: it is a three-voice composition in Tr88, as is the entire mass, but it is set for four voices in Tr90. The extra voice, labeled "tenor bassus," is clearly a filler, skipping around in a jagged line in its attempts to find the best note to double. Bedingham could have written this part, but it is more likely that someone else did him the service. Example 39 gives the beginning of this section as found in Tr90.

22 L. Feininger, <u>Monumenta</u> <u>Polyphoniae</u> <u>Liturgicae</u> <u>Sanctae</u> <u>Ecclesiae</u> <u>Romanae</u> (Rome, 1957), p. vii.

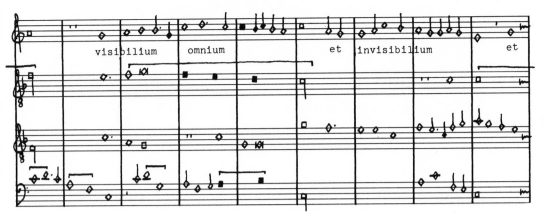

Musical Example 39: Patrem, _Missa_ _deul_ _angouisseux_ (Tr90 386'387)

The purpose of this brief excursion has been to point out that
even though there is close agreement on notational details among most of
the manuscripts of this period, Tr90 shows frequent and considerable variations from other sources. Either the scribe of Tr90 tampered with many
of the pieces as he copied them, to amuse himself or to get some practice
in composition, or he was copying from unusually inaccurate models. It is
unfortunate that the only manuscript preserving the _Missa_ _Sancti_ _Anthonii_
is less reliable in details than others of the time. Some of the many
deviations from Dufay's usual mensural practice may be the work of the
scribe, not the composer. But the deviations are so numerous that it seems
unlikely that they can all be blamed on the scribe. Besides, in all authentic Dufay works, of all periods, an almost obsessive desire to achieve
logical and even obvious formal organization by means of orderly patterns
of mensuration can be observed. This mass is not organized over a tenor;
it is not organized by means of motto beginnings in the various sections;
it is not organized by alternation of chant and polyphony, or "chorus" and
"duo" sections, or recurring mensural patterns. The mass in not organized
in any way that I am able to detect and thus I cannot imagine Dufay's
having written such a piece, at any period of his life.

Distinguishing characteristics: use of Φ with colored semiminims.

*Missa Sancti Anthonii

Kyrie:		(O) ¢ O
Et in terra:	superius	(O) ¢ $\frac{O}{3}$ ¢ 3 O Ꮯ (O) Ꮯ Ɔ 3 Φ
	tenor, contra	(O) ¢ O Φ
Patrem:	superius	(O) O ¢ Ɔ ¢ ¢ O3 (O) Ꮯ Φ
	tenor, contra	(O) O ¢ ¢ O
Sanctus:		(O) ¢
Agnus Dei:	superius	O ¢ 3 O
	tenor, contra	O ¢ O

Sanctus Tr92 216-217
  O O/C Φ O Φ O

Agnus Dei Tr92 217'218
  O Φ

Sanctus Papale
  O ¢ O ¢ O

Agnus custos et pastor
  O 3 O ¢ 3 ¢ O ¢ Φ

Et in terra de quaremiaulx
  superius, contra   O   Φ C
  tenor   O O Φ C ¢

Et in terra Tr92 144'146'
  Φ O ¢ Φ O

Et in terra Tr92 150'151
  Φ O

Sanctus BL 133
  O/C Φ O Φ O/C Φ O

Agnus Dei BL 134
  O Φ O

Fulgens iubar
  (O) C Φ

Juvenis qui puellam
  (O) ¢ O ¢ Φ Ꮯ (incomplete)

Magnanime gentis
  superius   O C 3 C Φ
  motetus   O C   Φ
  tenor   O C ¢   Φ

Nuper rosarum
  superius, contra   (O) ¢   Φ
  tenor   O C ¢ Φ

O proles yspanie
  Φ O Φ

Salve flos
  superius, contra   (O) Φ ¢   3 4
  tenor   O Φ C ¢

* Of questionable authenticity.

<u>Magnificat</u> <u>octavi</u> <u>toni</u>   <u>Si</u> <u>quereris</u> <u>miracula</u>
   O Φ O   (O) ¢ Φ C

<u>Vexilla</u> <u>regis</u>
   O Φ

CHAPTER 7
1433-<u>ca</u>. 1455

I have brought together as Group 7 all Dufay works in 0 throughout which use colored semiminims. These pieces, without exception, are
quite brief.

The use of colored semiminims establishes 1433 as the earliest
date any of the works in the group could have been written; their simplici-
ty of style and structure makes it difficult to determine a terminal date.
Dufay used fusae in pieces known to have been written late in his life, and
the presence of fusae in a composition is a clue that it is a late work,
but the absence of fusae in such simple pieces as those making up this
group may not be strong proof that they were written before a certain date.
Still, it is one of the few clues we have. I suggest a terminal date of
1455 for this group without feeling much assurance about this, for it could
easily be slightly later or even a great deal earlier. Most of the pieces
are found in Tr87, Tr92, BL and Ox—all manuscripts containing early and
middle Dufay works, but no late ones—and in the early chansonniers. The
one datable piece in the group, <u>Signeur Leon</u>, which Plamenac believes is by
Dufay and dates from 1444,[1] falls squarely in the middle of the suggested
period.

Some of these pieces are so similar to the works of Group 5 that
they must date from just about the same time. The two Kyries were not put
in Group 5 because they do not paraphrase any Gregorian Kyrie that I have
been able to locate; the hymns <u>Audi benigne</u> and <u>Criste redemptor</u> have the
chant melody in the tenor rather than the superius; the hymns <u>Ad cenam agni</u>
and <u>Festum nunc celebre</u> show no evidence of alternating chant and polyphony;
the two Benedicamus Domine settings found in ModB are written for three
voices, with the "Deo dicamus gratias" section in chant, but there is no
trace of chant paraphrase in the polyphonic sections. In all other respects
these pieces are similar to those in Group 5.

The <u>Kyrie in semiduplicibus maioribus</u> has music for one Kyrie,
one Criste, then one Kyrie, as do most of the Kyrie settings of this peri-
os, but there is an indication at the end of each of these three sections
that it is to be sung three times, giving it the traditional form of Kyrie
(three times), Criste (three times), Kyrie (three times). It is likely

---

[1] Dragan Plamenac, "An Unknown Composition by Dufay?" MQ, <u>40</u> (1954),
pp. 190-200.

that there was some variation in tempo when the sections were repeated, for
the sake of variety. The signatures ϕ and ϕ found in many Kyrie settings by Binchois—one of these is the <u>Kyrie</u> Tr87 56'57—must be his method
of recording a detail of performance practice which most composers did not
bother to notate.

All of the pieces in this group preserved in Ox are found in the
two latest fascicles, the first and fourth. Two of them, <u>Or pleust a Dieu</u>
and <u>Pouray je avoir</u>, use melodic figuration in the approach to a cadence
quite clearly related to the "English figure" referred to in earlier
chapters.

Musical Example 40: Dufay, <u>Or pleust a Dieu</u> (Ox 71')

I have suggested that there was contact between Dufay and English music
and/or musicians in 1433-1435; this is yet another bit of supporting evidence.

Breve coloration, with three colored breves or their equivalent
replacing two normal breves—usually in the tenor or the contra—is common
in pieces of this group. In the version of <u>Par le regart</u> found in Mel,
breve coloration is used in combination with minim coloration, with three
colored minims replacing two. The second and third colored breves are separated by a white minim and semibreve, making the passage even more complicated.

Musical Example 41: Dufay, <u>Par le regart</u> (Mel 73')

It would be simpler to explain the passage as two separate instances of
coloration, the first made up of two colored breves (or their equivalent)

and the second of two colored semibreves (or the equivalent)—the first being breve coloration and the second minim coloration—and to discard the
idea that there is separated coloration. The objection to this simplifica-
tion is that Dufay always uses coloration in multiples of three: passages
with semibreve coloration consist of three colored semibreves (or the equivalent) or some multiple, breve coloration is always made up of three colored
breves or a multiple, and so on. I have found no instance of Dufay's using
single colored notes which have lost a third of their value, though examples
can be found in pieces by other composers of the time.

Curiously, this passage in <u>Par le regart</u> does not use coloration
in Lab, where the colored semibreve—colored minim figure is replaced by a
dotted semibreve and a minim. Even more curious, the passage is not correct
in Lab. (See Ex. 41) The third semibreve in this version should be altered,
according to the rules of mensural notation, but the passage does not come
out as it should if this is done. Mel is clearer: the coloration prevents
alteration.

The motet <u>Veni delicti</u> is attributed to Dufay in Tr87 and to Lymburgia in BL; it is such a simple piece that it is difficult to find anything in its notational usage pointing to one composer or the other. But
in an earlier chapter, I extracted a number of cadential figures from a
piece by Lymburgia and pointed out how carefully he avoided exact repeti-
tion of the same figure. This peculiarity can be noted in other Lymburgia
works, wheras Dufay is usually content to use the same figure over and over
again.

Musical Example 42: Dufay-Lymburgia, <u>Veni dilecti</u> (BL 301[b])

Example 42 gives the superius part leading to the nine cadences of <u>Veni
dilecti</u>; no two are alike, although the third and fifth differ in only one
note, and if either Dufay or Lymburgia wrote the piece it must have been
the latter.

THE WORKS OF GROUP 7
1433-<u>ca</u>. 1455

    <u>Distinguishing characteristics</u>: use of tempus perfectum only, with colored semiminims and no fusae.

<u>Kyrie in Dominicis diebus</u>
(O)

<u>Kyrie in semiduplicibus maioribus</u>
(O)

*<u>Veni dilecti</u>
(O)

<u>Ad cenam agni</u>
O

<u>Benedicamus Domino</u> BL 169[b]
(O)

<u>Audi benigne</u>
(O)

<u>Criste redemptor</u>
(O)

<u>Benedicamus Domino</u> BL 114
(O)

<u>Festum nunc celebre</u>
(O)

<u>Adieu quitte le demeurant</u>
(O)

<u>Craindre vous vueil</u>
(O)

<u>Bien doy servir</u>
(O)

<u>Dona gentile bella</u>
(O)

<u>Ce jour le doibt</u>
(O)

<u>Donnez l'assault</u>
(O)

* Probably by Lymburgia.

120

En languir en piteux
(O)

Entre les plus plaines
O

Je nay deubta fors
(O)

Je prens congie
(O)

Las que feray
(O)

Mille bonjours
O

Mon bien m'amour
(O)

Or pleust a Dieu
(O)

Par le regart
(O)

Pouray je avoir
(O)

Puisque celle qui me tient en prison
(O)

Qu'est devenue
(O)

Se la face
(O)

Seigneur Leon
O

Trop lonc temps
(O)

Va ten mon cuer
(O)

Vo regart et doulche maniere
(O)

   Group 8 contains those Dufay compositions which use the mensuration O with ₵, ₵3 or C, or which use one of the latter alone, which
have colored semiminims, and which contain no fusae. The group overlaps
with both Group 6 and Group 7, differing from the former in that it does
not use ₵, and from the latter in that mensurations in addition to, or in-
stead of, O are used.

   The use of ₵ gives a date of 1435 as one boundary, but once
again there is difficulty in establishing a terminal date. The motet
<u>Mirandas</u> <u>parit</u>, with a text in praise of Florence and the young virgins of
that city, must date from 1435-1436; <u>Moribus</u> <u>et</u> <u>genere</u>, in honor of St.
John and apparently composed for Dijon, may date from Dufay's visit to this
city in 1446; and <u>O</u> <u>tres</u> <u>piteulx</u>, a lament on the fall of Constantinople,
was written in 1453 or 1454 and performed at the Banquet of the Pheasant at
Lille in 1454. The dates of these three pieces and the absence of fusae
are the best guides to establishing the period in which the pieces of this
group were written. I have added a few years to the date of the latest
datable work, though my suggestion of 1460 as the terminal year carries no
great conviction.

   O and ₵ are the basic mensurations, and the two seem to have
been thought of as being in a 2:1 proportion to one another, as was the
case in the pieces of Group 6. Dufay never used the two mensurations
against one another,[1] but there is such a complete shift from semibreve-
minim movement in O to breve-semibreve movement in ₵ that it is not necessary to look at the signature to tell which of the two is in use. A
count of movement confirms this shift of values:

		longs	breves	semibreves	minims	semiminims
<u>Kyrie</u>	O	12	40	127	123	25
Tr92 144[2]	₵	10	51	59	18	-
<u>Ave</u> <u>regina</u>	O	11	65	179	235	20
ModB 59'60	₵	26	125	161	14	-

---

[1] Though other composers of the time did. The anonymous <u>Salve</u> <u>regina</u>
(ModB 69) has O in the superius and tenor against ₵ in the contra. A
breve of ₵ equals a semibreve of O.

[2] This <u>Kyrie</u> is written in psuedo-score. I did not put it in Group 5

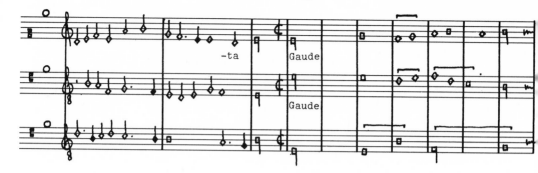

Musical Example 43: Dufay, Ave regina celorum (Tr88 327'328)

Example 43 illustrates one of the common cadences of this time, in which a prepared dissonance resolves to the penultimate note of the cadence. This dissonance has the duration of a minim in O and a semibreve in ¢, another indication that the two mensurations were thought of as being in something approaching a 2:1 ratio to one another.

Tempus imperfectum moves in breves and semibreves in most of these works, whether under the signature ¢ or C. I take the two signatures to mean the same thing, C being found in only a few pieces where ¢ seems implied, such as Hic vir despiciens, O gemma martirum, and several other antiphon settings which are all found in one section of ModB. Since C here is equivalent to ¢, the use of the cipher 3 has the same effect as in ¢: three semibreves replace two, giving the same organization as that of tempus perfectum. But there is a tempo difference between O and ¢3. Assuming a breve of ¢ to be equal to a semibreve of O, then three semibreves of ¢3 will equal one of O.

There is also apparent equivalence between ¢3 and ¢ with semibreve coloration. Both have three semibreves to the breve and must move at the same speed, since both are dependent on the tempo of ¢ itself. But in the Dufay works it is always possible to see why one was used rather than the other. The superius of Moribus et genere, for example, has several sections in ¢ with semibreve coloration and several other sections in ¢3. In both ¢3 sections semiminims are used, these notes being made as colored minims; if these sections had been in coloration there would be no way to distinguish between minims and semiminims, unless another color of ink had been used for the semiminims. The contra part of this motet also has two passages in ¢3, and coloration is used in both. Again, there would have been no way of showing this if the entire passage had been in coloration.

_____

because the superius does not paraphrase a Gregorian Kyrie and because the mensuration ¢ was not used in other pieces in this group. The piece is found in Ca6 and Ca11, which could be another clue that pseudo-score layout has something to do with France—assuming that these two manuscripts originated from Cambrai.

In both instances we see Dufay achieving the effect of coloration of coloration by using coloration and a cipher, just as he did in certain earlier
works.

Often there is a more basic reason for the use of ₵ with colora-
tion rather than ₵3. Example 44, a fragment of the superius of <u>Moribus</u> <u>et</u>
<u>genere</u>, illustrates a type of passage in ₵-coloration which could not have
been notated in ₵3.

Musical Example 44: Dufay, <u>Moribus</u> <u>et</u> <u>genere</u> (ModB 75'76)

Three semibreves replace two normal semibreves, just as in ₵3, but the
distinctive rhythm of the passage derives from the replacement of two normal breves by three colored ones. This is not semibreve coloration, but
breve coloration.

Sub-group 8[a] contains the handful of works in which tempus imperfectum moves in semibreves and minims under the signature C, rather than
with the usual breve-semibreve movement found under both C and ₵. It
contains two major and interesting works, the <u>Missa</u> <u>caput</u> and the <u>Missa</u> <u>se</u>
<u>la</u> <u>face</u>.

We know that the <u>Kyrie</u> of the <u>Missa</u> <u>caput</u> was copied in Cambrai
in 1463,[3] and until quite recently this date was taken to be the date of
composition of the mass. But Bukofzer, in his last discussion of the piece,
admitted that a date somewhere in the 1450's would be more comfortable,[4]
and even more recently, Besseler has suggested that it must date from the
time of Dufay's "intercourse with English musicians,"[5] which he places in
the neighborhood of 1440.

Notationally, the use of colored semiminims places the work after
1433—not that there was any question about this. A count of movement in
O and C shows that there is not the shift of values between tempus perfectum and tempus imperfectum found in most pieces of this group:[6]

---

[3] J. Houdoy, <u>Histoire</u> <u>artistique</u> <u>de</u> <u>la</u> <u>cathédrale</u> <u>de</u> <u>Cambrai</u> (Paris, 1880),
p. 194.
[4] Bukofzer, "<u>Caput</u> <u>Redivivum</u>," pp. 97-110.
[5] Besseler (ed.), <u>Opera</u> <u>Omnia</u>, III, p. iii.
[6] All sources but Tr90 (and Tr93, a copy of it) agree on these signatures;
these two have ₵ for the three middle sections. Mention has been made of
the unreliability of Tr90, and disagreements of this sort between it and
other more reliable sources should cast no doubt on the readings of the
latter.

		longs	breves	semibreves	minims	semiminims
Kyrie	O	2	18	108	163	26
Christe	C	4	36	109	90	7

There is a slight shift in the direction of larger notes in C, but nothing approaching the complete shift to breve-semibreve movement usually found in ¢.

The Missa caput is a tenor mass, probably the first of this type written by Dufay. The current opinion is that the tenor mass originated with English composers, that it evolved from the isorhythmic motet, and that two of the earliest preserved masses of this type are the Missa alma redemptoris and the Missa rex seculorum, both attributed to Leonel Power. If he did write them, they must date from before 1445, the year of his death.

The Missa caput was quite probably based on an English model. Bukofzer demonstrated that the cantus firmus was taken from the final melisma of the Sarum version of the antiphon Venit ad Petrum, and it seems more likely that some English composer selected this cantus for a tenor for a mass which Dufay took as a model than that Dufay himself selected this particular bit of chant. The notion that Dufay's Missa caput had some connection with England has been strengthened by the discovery of fragments of this mass in an English manuscript.[7]

Notationally, there are hints that the mass has something to do with English music. And even though the English Missa caput, if there was one, has not turned up, one does not have to search far for an English mass which resembles Dufay's Missa caput so closely that it must be at least a cousin, if not a parent. It is none other than the Leonel Power Missa alma redemptoris. The similarity between the two is apparent first of all from a comparison of the basic mensuration pattern of the two:

Power, Missa alma redemptoris   Dufay, Missa caput

                                        Kyrie   O
                                        Christe   C

Et in terra   O   Et in terra O
Qui tollis   C   Qui tollis   C

_____

[7] But see Ruth Hannas, "Concerning Deletions in the Polyphonic Mass Credo," JAMS, 5 (1952), pp. 155-186, for a dissenting opinion. Miss Hannas connects the selection of this particular cantus firmus with a religious and political controversy, suggests that Dufay wrote the mass in 1440 for the coronation of Amadeus VIII of Savoy as Pope Felix V, and denies any English involvement in the matter.

Patrem	O	Patrem	O
Qui ex patre	C	Et incarnatus	C
Sanctus	O	Sanctus	O
Pleni sunt	O	Pleni sunt	O
Benedictus	C	Benedictus	C
Agnus Dei	O	Agnus Dei	O
Agnus Dei	O	Agnus Dei	O
Agnus Dei	C	Agnus Dei	C

Power telescopes the portion of the text beginning with "Et ex patre" in the superius with the portion beginning "Crucifixus" in the contra. This telescoping continues to the beginning of the section in tempus imperfectum, which begins with "Qui ex patre." There is no telescoping in the Dufay. The superius stops at the same place in the text before the section in tempus imperfectum as did Power's superius, but since Dufay has not telescoped his text, the section in C begins with "Et incarnatus."

Another similarity between the two is the use of a mensuration—C with semibreve-minim movement—not normally found in the works of either, at this period. With the exception of a few simple, and I assume early, settings of mass sections found in OH, Power's tempus imperfectum moves in breves and semibreves, whether the signature in a particular manuscript be C or ¢. The other tenor mass attributed to him, the Missa rex seculorum, has breve-semibreve movement in tempus imperfectum.

A comparison of the layout of the tenors of the two masses reveals similar but not identical organization:

Missa alma redemptoris

			A		B		C			D		E		F
Et in terra	O		16	(4)	16	(8)	14	C		20	(8)	38	(8)	12
Patrem	O	(36)	16	(4)	16	(8)	14	C	(18)	20	(8)	38	(8)	12
Sanctus	O	(9)	16	(4)	16	(8)	14	C		20	(8)	38	(8)	12
Agnus Dei	O		16	(4)	16	(8)	14	C		20	(8)	38	(8)	12

Missa caput

			A		B		C		D				E		F
Kyrie	O	(21)	30	(4)	12	(9)	16	(1)	12	C	(40)	46	(20)	44
Et in terra	O	(16)	30	(1)	12	(2)	16	(1)	12	C	(38)	90	(E + F)	
Patrem	O	(19)	30	(2)	12	(3)	16	(1)	12	C	(56)	46	(16)	44
Sanctus	O	(17)	30	(4)	12	(3)	14	(1)	12	C	(24)	46	(6)	44
Agnus Dei	O	(16)	30	(4)	12	(4)	16	(1)	12	C	(20)	32	(4)	32

Power has broken his tenor into three segments in each half of each of the four sections, always maintaining the same number of rests between each segment of the tenor from one section to the next. The only structural freedom he allowed himself was in the use of introductory measures before the first entrance of the tenor in the Patrem and Sanctus. Dufay also split his tenor into six fragments, four for the first section of each movement and two for the second. He allowed himself freedom not only in the length of the sections before the entrance of the tenor, but also in the number of measures between any of the fragments of his cantus firmus. Both composers chopped up their chant <u>cantus</u> <u>firmus</u> in an apparently arbitrary way, ignoring phrasing and cadences.

Another hint that the <u>Missa</u> <u>caput</u> had something to do with English music is the repeated use of the "English figure" throughout the work. I have pointed out that this melodic turn can be found only in English works and in a handful of other pieces probably influenced by English music.

Musical Example 45: Dufay, <u>Missa</u> <u>caput</u> (Agnus Dei III, Tr89 255'256)

I have been able to find the figure in only two other Dufay works, Or pleust a Dieu and Pouray je avoir, both of which were probably written around 1435 and must reflect Dufay's contact with English music at this time. The figure runs through the Missa caput almost like a leitmotif, appearing not only in its simplest form just before cadences but also in many other guises throughout the mass, often in sequential patterns. It seems as though Dufay used this figure, so characteristic of English music, as a symbol of his indebtedness to the model or models of the Missa caput.

This mass is similar in so many ways to the Power Missa alma redemptoris that it is difficult to escape the conclusion that one was modeled after the other, though this does not explain why the composer who wrote his mass first made the departure from his usual mensural practice in using tempus imperfectum with semibreve-minim movement. Another possibility is that both were modeled on a mass by still another composer, for whom C with semibreve-minim movement was a normal mensuration, but such a mass has not been discovered. Unless more English manuscripts of the period are found, it will be impossible to say whether the likenesses between the Power and Dufay masses come from the direct influence of one on the other, or whether there was only indirect contact, by way of still another mass, between the two.

Notationally, Dufay's Missa se la face is a twin to the Missa caput. It is found in Tr88 in the same hand which inserted the Missa caput in Tr89, it uses only the two mensurations O and C with semibreve-minim movement in both, and there are colored semiminims but no fusae. The tenor is augmented, not by the use of major prolation in the tenor, but by canon: the instruction for the Kyrie, Sanctus and Agnus Dei is "Crescit in duplo," for the Et in terra and Patrem it is "Primo quelibet figura crescit in triplo, secundo in duplo, tertio ut jacet." Contrary to the basic organization of the Missa caput, here there is a tripartite structure for each section but the Sanctus:

Dufay, Missa se la face

Kyrie	O	Et in terra	O	Patrem	O
Christe	C	Qui tollis	C	Et iterum	C
Kyrie	O	Cum sancto	O	Confiteor	O

Sanctus	O		Agnus Dei	O
Pleni sunt	(O)		Agnus Dei	C
Osanna	(O)		Agnus Dei	O
Benedictus	C			
Osanna	(C)			

This mass and the Missa caput must date from about the same time, judging from notational similarities. This must be after 1433-1435, because

of the use of colored semiminims, and before the works in Group 9, because
of the absence of fusae. Thus we can verify Besseler's assertion that
these are Dufay's two earliest tenor masses, since all others of this type
fall in Group 9. The two are exceptional in their use of C with semibreve-
minim movement and for this reason are difficult to fit into a chronology
based on his usual practice.

Three other works belong in sub-group 8^a because of their use of
C with semibreve-minim movement: the _Magnificat primi toni_, _Ma plus
mignonne_, and _Puis que vous estez campieur_. The Magnificat is mostly in O,
with three verses in C; it is probably not by Dufay. His name appears at
the beginning of the piece in ModB, but Binchois' name is then inserted at
the top of the "Et exultavit" verse as though it were a correction of the
initial ascription, or as though only the first verse were by Dufay and the
remainder of the piece by Binchois. The work is anonymous in SPB80; the
first verse, the one attributed to Dufay in ModB, has been replaced in this
manuscript by an altogether different setting, though the other verses correspond to those in ModB. The work is apparently by Binchois, with a setting of the "Et exultavit" verse by Dufay replacing Binchois' original verse
in ModB.

Dufay deviated from his normal mensural practice (¢ or C with
breve-semibreve movement) in the two masses in Group 8^a because he was using a work by another composer as a model. It is not clear why he used an
unusual mensuration in the three shorter works in this group. Perhaps they
were written at the same time as the masses. Perhaps they too were modeled
on other works, though there is no evidence of this. Or it may be that all
five works in Group 8^a date from quite early in the period I have suggested
for the group, from just after 1435, at a time when Dufay had not as yet
abandoned C for ¢.

Two short secular works, _De partes vous male bouche_ and _Dieu gard
la bone_, are exceptional in that they use ¢ with semibreve-minim movement.
A count of the first gives:

	longs	breves	semibreves	minims	semiminims
¢	1	9	56	50	4

I have put these two in additional sub-group 8^b. The use of ¢ (semibreve-
minim) is even more at variance with Dufay's normal practice than is the use
of C(semibreve-minim) in the works of Group 8^a, being found nowhere else,
either earlier or later.

There are three possible explanations for this mensuration. The
scribe may have mistakenly copied ¢ for C; I have pointed out on several
occasions that the only common error in notational details among scribes of
the time was the omission of the stroke through a signature, or the addition

of such a stroke when it was not found in the model from which the copying
was being done. A second possibility is that the two pieces are not by
Dufay, but were written by someone for whom ₵ (semibreve-minim) was a normal mensuration. Another explanation, the one that I am inclined to accept,
is that the works are authentic, but date from a later period than the other
works in my eighth group. The distinguishing characteristic of Group 9 is
the use of fusae, but even though it is clear enough that Dufay used notes
of this small value only toward the end of his career, he may not have used
fusae in all works written at this time. The situation is similar to one I
mentioned in an earlier chapter: the works of Group 1 have no semiminims,
but there are probably a handful of pieces dating from this time which do,
exceptionally, use semiminims and therefore do not fall in this group. The
clue that the two pieces in Group 8^b probably date from the end of Dufay's
life is the use of ₵ (semibreve-minim). As will be pointed out in the
next chapter, a trend toward movement in smaller notes in all mensurations
can be seen in his last works. Movement in ₵, which had been so clearly
in breves and semibreves in works from his middle periods, shades to breve-
semibreve-minim movement, and finally approaches semibreve-minim.

Even though De partes vous male bouche and Dieu gard la bone fit
in my eighth group because of their lack of fusae, I place them in the last
decade or two of Dufay's life.

Laurence Feininger has published eleven cycles of polyphonic settings of propers which he attributes to Dufay.[8] They comprise sixty-five
separate pieces, they are all found in Tr88, and every one of the sixty-
five is anonymous in this manuscript. They are:

Missa de spiritu sancto	Tr88 113'121
Missa de S.S. trinitate	121'128
Missa de S. Andrea apostolo	128'134
Missa de S. cruce	135'140'
Missa de S. Joanne baptista	141'147
Missa de angelis	147'154
Missa de S. Georgi	154'161'
Missa de S. Mauritii et Sociorum	169'176
Missa de S. Anthonii de Padua	182'189
Missa de S. Francisci	189'193'
Missa de S. Sebastiani	210'215'

Feininger offers the following reasons for attributing all this
music to Dufay:

1. Tr88 is the unique source for these cycles, but three single

---

[8] Feininger, Monumenta, Series II, Tomus I, 1947.

pieces, detached from their cycles, are found in Tr90. One of these, the
Alleluia veni sancte spiritus, is attributed to Dufay on Tr90 420.

2. The cycles, intermingled with six other proper cylces which
Feininger does not believe are by Dufay, are arranged in what appears to
be liturgical order in Tr88. He has found structural details which convince
him that the eleven masses listed above are by one and the same composer:
note-for-note correspondence can be observed in entire passages in various
pairs and groups. Since one piece is attributed to Dufay elsewhere, he
attributes the remaining sixty-four to the same composer.

3. He states that he has made a close stylistic study of all the
music in these cycles, all other music attributed to Dufay, and all music
by Dufay's contemporaries, which has convinced him that only Dufay could
have written the cycles. Unfortunately, the promised monograph detailing
the findings of this comprehensive stylistic study has not yet appeared.

Feininger may be correct. All this music may be by Dufay. It
would go beyond the limits of this book for me to comment on stylistic features of these pieces or even to dwell on what is certainly the weakest
link in his chain of reasoning, the ascription of sixty-five anonymous compositions to one composer on the basis of the attribution of one similar
piece (in a somewhat different form, incidentally) in a manuscript notorious
for its inaccuracies. I will merely point out that the two most common mensurations in the pieces which make up these cycles are O with semibreve-
minim movement and C with breve-semibreve movement, that in a few of them
the signature ₵ is used in what seems to be an interchangeable way with C,
that the pieces contain no fusae, and that therefore, if Dufay did write
this music it belongs in my Group 8 and must date from the period 1435-1460.

But, more important, my entire study is based on the assumption
that Dufay used only a limited number of signatures and mensurations, using
these consistently and repeatedly—and two signatures found in no pieces
ascribed to Dufay, C2 and O2, are used in these cycles:

C2	Introit Dum sanctificatus	Tr88 121'122
	Alleluia Verbo Domini	125'126
	Introit Michi autem	128'129
	Gradual Benedicite Dominum	148'150

C2	Introit Nos autem	Tr88 135'136
	Alleluia In conspectu	150'151
	Offertory Stetit angelus	152'153
	Gradual Gloriosus Deus	171'173
	Gradual Os justi	183'185

C2 signals a mensuration in duple organization throughout, with
two semibreves to the breve and two minims to the semibreve. Theorists
classify this signature as one calling for a duple proportion and equate it

with ¢. In the manuscript in which these cycles are found, C2 and ¢
seem to mean the same thing in practice: Tr88 58'59, an anonymous <u>Sanctus</u>,
has one voice in C2 against another in ¢, and from a transcription we
see that the two are equivalent; exactly the same situation is found in the
anonymous <u>Agnus Dei</u> which follows immediately; the four sections of the
Bedingham <u>Missa deul angouisseux</u> have a signature of C2 in Tr88, but ¢ in
Tr90. In addition, the three signatures C, ¢, and C2 appear to be interchangeable in the cycles of propers attributed to Dufay by Feininger. Movement under all three is in breves and semibreves: C is found in one voice
against C2 in another in the introit <u>Michi autem</u>, on Tr88 128'129, and in
the communion <u>Venite post me</u> (Tr88 134'), ¢ in one voice proves to be equivalent to C in another.

        C2, then, which is never found in works attributed to Dufay in
manuscripts of the period, calls for a mensuration found in his works under
another signature. The sections in these cycles under the signature O2,
however, are in a genuinely different mensuration from any found in the
Dufay works, one in which the long is divided into three breves, the breve
into two semibreves, and the semibreve into two minims. It could be described as tempus perfectum with all values shifted one place to the left.

        Certain twentieth-century scholars have had difficulty in compre-
hending the difference between Φ and O2; some have even been under the
impression that the two were equivalent. It is true that in a few pieces
dating from the period of pseudo-augmentation O2 was used to signal a
faster beat in tempus perfectum, to equate it with another voice in major
prolation, as was Φ. But after the first third of the century there was a
clear distinction between Φ, organized 2, 3, 2, and O2, organized 3, 2, 2.

        Tact tables tell us that the beat was on the semibreve in O and
on the breve in O2. If the beat were to go at the same rate of speed in
the two, the effect of the two mensurations would be exactly the same to
the ear, since O2 has the same organization as O, at the next higher level
of organization. This is another of the puzzling cases of two mensurations
written differently, yet apparently sounding the same.

        The <u>Missa de angelis</u> (Tr88 147'154) has the mensuration scheme:

Introit	C			
Gradual	superius, contra	C2	3	C
	tenor	(C)		
Alleluia	superius, contra	(C)	3	C
	tenor	O2		
Alleluia	(C)			
Offertory	(O2)	3	O2	
Communion	C3	C		

Movement in all mensurations is in breves and semibreves. C and C2 are

equivalent: the gradual begins with C2 in the two upper voices, changes
briefly to (C 2)3, then to C, and since both C and C2 are in the same
relationship to the tenor, which remains in one mensuration, they must be
equal to one another. The cipher 3 in the course of a section in C or C2
has the effect of replacing two semibreves by three, just as it does in the
course of O2. In all, four mensurations appear in the cycle:[9]

C (= C 2)	2, 2, 2
O2	3, 2, 2
C3	2, 3, 2
(O 2)3	3, 3, 2

These are nothing more than the four most common mensurations of the time
written at the next level of mensuration:

C	2, 2, 2
O	2, 3, 2
C3	2, 2, 3
(O)3	2, 3, 3

Tact tables from the end of the century say that the beat in each
of the mensurations in the second group was on the semibreve. The beat in
C 2 and O2 was said to be on the breve, and if this was so it must have
been on the breve also in C3 and (O 2)3. Thus, the entire Missa de
angelis is written in four mensurations which can be thought of as four
common mensurations of the time written at the next level of mensuration,
with notes twice as large and with the beat on the next highest note, sounding exactly the same to the ear as the more common mensurations.

Why are the cycles written this way? They are made up of quite
simple pieces, possibly because longer, more elaborate pieces would not
have been appropriate, liturgically. It is also possible that the singers
available for the performance of this music were not of the caliber of the
singers who made up the Papal Choir, for example, and that the composer of
these cycles kept the limitations of his performers in mind. Poor musicians
tend to panic at the sight of too many black notes. It is not impossible
that whoever wrote this music thought that his singers would be more comfortable with music moving in breves, semibreves, and minims than in semibreves, minims, and semiminims.

Another mensuration, O with semibreve-minim movement, is used
in several of the cycles. This contrasts with the breve-semibreve movement
of the other mensurations and the beat was probably on the semibreve, not

---

[9] Here, and elsewhere, I show the organization of a particular mensuration
by a set of three numbers indicating modus, tempus, and prolation. "2, 3, 2"
means two breves to a long (modus), two semibreves to a breve (tempus), and
two minims to a semibreve (prolation).

on the breve as elsewhere in this music. Here again a parallel can be
drawn between this and the more common mensural practice: ₵ was still used
occasionally around the turn of the century, mostly by provincial composers,
and movement in this mensuration tended to be in smaller notes (minim-
semiminim movement, as opposed to the semibreve-minim movement in the more
common mensurations), with a beat on the next smallest note (minim) rather
than the one (semibreve) on which it usually fell.

          O2, as used in these cycles, carries the implication that diminu-
tion is to take place, but the signature does not invariably call for such
diminution in other works of the period. Tr89 273'281 is an anonymous mass
using this signature in all voices throughout all five sections, but even
though organization under O2 is the same as in the proper cycles discussed
above, movement is in semibreves and minims. Here the signature does not
call for diminution, but merely for a rhythmic organization different from
that found under the more usual signatures, one which could be transcribed
best into modern notation as 3/2.

          In the publications in the series in which he offers the "Dufay"
proper cycles, Feininger breaks with the current trend in publication of
old music by offering an edition with all voices in their original clefs,
unreduced in value and with original signatures. Half bar lines mark off
tempus and modus; ligatures and coloration are indicated; and he even makes
clear such details as the type of semiminim used in the original manuscript.
This is anything but a "practical" edition and would seem to eliminate the
necessity of going to original sources of this music.

          But even though a check of Feininger's edition reveals that he
has been accurate in general, it also turns up discrepancies. In some
pieces, conflicting signatures—C in one voice against ₵ or C2 in another,
for example—have been arbitrarily eliminated and all voices given the same
signature, with no indication of the original reading. And in some pieces
he has made even more drastic changes in signatures, again without informing
the reader that he is departing from the original:
          1. The Alleluia verbo Domino (Tr88 125'126) has a mensural pat-
tern of C2 3 O2 in the superius against O2 in the other two voices, but
Feininger has O2 for all three voices, throughout.
          2. The introit Michi autem (Tr88 128'129) has C2 for the versus
and doxology, Feininger has O2.
          3. The Alleluia dulce lignum (Tr88 138'139) has O2 3 C in the
superius against O2 in the tenor and contra, Feininger has C in all voices.
          4. The Alleluia in conspectu (Tr88 150'151) has O2 in the tenor
against C in the other two voices, Feininger has C in all voices.

          Perhaps Feininger had sound reasons for making changes such as
these. But the fact that he made them without informing the reader that he
was deviating from what is found in the manuscript raises the possibility

that there are other unadvertised deviations in the edition and makes it
necessary for anyone engaged in detailed work on these cycles to go to the
manuscripts after all.

These cycles are in a world of mensural practice quite different
from that of Dufay. I cannot accept them as works of this composer.

The attribution of anonymous works to Dufay has become a popular
pastime, one of the attractions of the sport being that it is difficult to
prove, on stylistic grounds, that a particular anonymous piece is not by
Dufay. Zest is given to the game by the strong possibility that some Dufay
works are indeed preserved as anonymous compositions.

It will be noticed that my groups become smaller as they progress
chronologically. According to my findings, Dufay wrote much more music in
the first twenty or twenty-five years of his career than he did in the last
three or four decades of his life. It may be that he simply wrote less
music as he aged; after all, he was at least in his mid-seventies when he
died. But there is no sign of diminution of his ability to write well in
those works known to come from the end of his life. And it is also true
that the manuscript situation in the middle third of the century is quite
bad, particularly in regard to sacred music.

A considerable number of manuscripts from the period up to about
1440 have been preserved, and concordances of Dufay works between these
sources are so numerous that there is no question that a large percentage
of the music he wrote up to this time has come down to us. A few years ago,
a large codex from this period was discovered, the manuscript Ao, and even
though it contained more pieces by Dufay than any other composer, every one
of these was already known from other manuscripts. Also, most sources from
this period are quite good in the number of composer attributions, and even
though there is occasional disagreement between manuscripts as to who wrote
a particular piece, there is no reason to suspect that any significant number of Dufay works have come down to us as anonymous pieces or have been
hidden under the name of some other composer.

But we have fewer manuscripts from the period 1440-1480; the Dufay
works in them are frequently unique to the single source in which they are
preserved; and composer attributions are distressingly scattered. SPB80
dates from this period, for example, and on its 248 folios are only four
composer attributions—three of the four being later additions. The manuscript contains such late Dufay works as the motet Ave regina celorum and
the mass based on this motet; we know that these are by Dufay only because
of concordances with other manuscripts, or from some external evidence.
This situation raises the question of whether certain of the other anonymous
works in the manuscript are by Dufay and have not been identified as such

because they are unique to SPB 80, or because they are anonymous also in other manuscripts.

I would like to call attention to one of the anonymous masses in this manuscript, SPB80 113'121. Its organization is:

Kyrie	O	Et in terra	O	Patrem	O
Christe	¢	Qui tollis	¢	Et in spiritum	¢
Kyrie	O	Cum sancto	O	Et vitam	O

Sanctus	O	Agnus Dei	O
Pleni sunt	O	Agnus Dei	¢
Osanna	O	Agnus Dei	O
Benedictus	¢		
Osanna	O		

Movement in O is in semibreves and minims, with some colored semiminims, and there is breve-semibreve movement under ¢ with no semiminims. There is no external evidence suggesting that the mass is by Dufay, but mensural organization and usage are identical to that found in his works of Group 8, and the mass is preserved in a source containing late Dufay works. An interesting feature of the mass is that each of the five sections is related by a motto beginning, and a second motto begins the ¢ section of each.

It is generally agreed that Dufay took over the technique of the tenor mass from English composers and enriched it by the use of motto beginnings. His earliest tenor masses use rather extended mottos in the two upper voices, and all five sections of the late <u>Missa</u> <u>ave</u> <u>regina</u> <u>celorum</u> have identical beginnings for the first eight tempora in all voices. Masses written in the 1420's and 1430's by continental composers show some use of the motto technique. The unanswered question is whether Dufay developed this technique before he began writing tenor masses, or whether the two techniques were developed simultaneously.

Assuming with Besseler that the first Dufay tenor masses date from around 1440, there is a gap of almost fifteen years between these and the earlier <u>Missa</u> <u>sine</u> <u>nomine</u> and <u>Missa</u> <u>Sancti</u> <u>Jacobi</u>. The <u>Missa</u> <u>Sancti</u> <u>Anthonii</u>, if it is by Dufay, must date from about the middle of this gap, but it shows no refinement of motto technique over the two earliest masses. The anonymous mass in SPB80, mentioned above, could date from 1440, or even a few years earlier. It is not a tenor mass, but it exhibits rather refined use of motto technique. If it could be proved that the mass is by Dufay—and from what I have been able to assimilate about his style, he might well have written it—it would fill a gap in our knowledge of the history of the development of the cyclic mass.

1435-<u>ca</u>. 1460

Distinguishing characteristics: use of O and ¢ (with breve-
semibreve movement) as basic mensurations, colored simiminims and no fusae.

<u>Kyrie</u> Tr92 144
O ¢ O

<u>Ave regina celorum</u> Tr88 327'329   <u>O tres piteulx</u>
  O ¢ O   O ¢

<u>Mirandas parit</u>   <u>Salve regina</u>
  O ¢   O ¢ O ¢

<u>Moribus et genere</u>   *<u>O sidus yspanie</u>
  superius, motetus (O) ¢ 3 ¢ 3 ¢   O ¢
  tenor, contra   O C ¢

<u>O gloriose tyro</u>
  superius, motetus,
    contra   O ¢
  tenor   O C

<u>Magnificat sexti toni</u>
O ¢ O ¢ O ¢

<u>Aures ad nostram</u>   <u>Hic vir despiciens</u>
  ¢   C

<u>Alleluia veni sancte spiritus</u>   <u>Magi videntes</u>
  ¢   C3

* Anonymous, attributed to Dufay.

<u>O gemma martirum</u>
C

<u>Salve nos Domine</u>
¢

<u>Petrus apostolus</u>
¢

<u>Salve sancte pater</u>
C 3 C

<u>Proles de celo</u>
C

<u>Sapiente filio pater</u>
¢

<u>Propter nimiam</u>
¢

<u>Adieu m'amour</u>
¢

<u>Ne je ne dors</u>
¢

<u>Belle vueilles moy vengier</u>
¢3

<u>S'il est plaisir</u>
O ¢

THE WORKS OF GROUP 8[a]
1435-<u>ca</u>. 1460

<u>Distinguishing characteristics</u>: use of O and C (with semibreve-minim movement) as basic mensurations, colored semiminims and no fusae.

<u>Missa caput</u>			<u>Missa se la face</u>		
Kyrie	O	C	Kyrie	O C O
Et in terra	O	C	Et in terra	O C O
Patrem	O	C	Patrem	O C O
Sanctus	O	C	Sanctus	O C
Agnus Dei	O	C	Agnus Dei	O C O

[*]<u>Magnificat primi toni</u>
O C O

<u>Je vous pri</u>
C

<u>Ma plus mignonne</u>
C

<u>Puis que vous estez campieur</u>
C

* Of questionable authenticity.

THE WORKS OF GROUP 8[b]

<u>ca</u>. 1454-1474

   <u>Distinguishing characteristics</u>: use of ₵ with semibreve-minim movement, colored semibreve and no fusae.

<u>Magnificat tertii toni</u>

○ ₵ ○

<u>De partes vous male bouche</u>
₵

<u>Dieu gard la bone</u>
₵3

CHAPTER 9
ca. 1454-1474

I have put all compositions by Dufay with fusae in this, my last
group. This criterion alone brings together all works known to have been
written late in his life: the Missa ecce ancilla was copied at Cambrai by
the scribe Simon Mellet in the year 1463 and is assumed to date from this
year or shortly before;[1] the motet Ave regina celorum SPB80 25'27 was
copied by the same scribe the following year;[2] the Missa ave regina celorum
is built on this piece and probably dates from 1464 or later; the handful
of secular songs is preserved only in manuscripts dating from the end of
the century. There can be no quarrel with 1474 as the terminal date, but
the date at the other end is difficult to fix.

We know that a "song" with the title Je ne vis oncques la pareille
was sung at the Banquet of the Oath of the Pheasant in Lille in 1454.[3] A
rondeau with a first line beginning with these words is found in a number
of manuscripts, and in one it is attributed to Dufay. Fusae are used;
thus if this is the piece sung at the banquet, and if it is by Dufay, the
first date for the group must be pushed back at least to 1454. The identification of this piece with the one sung at the banquet is not certain,
however, and since it is ascribed to Binchois in one manuscript, we cannot
be certain it is by Dufay. And O tres piteulx, which was sung at the banquet and is almost certainly by Dufay, makes no use of fusae. For want of
other evidence, though, I will suggest 1454 as the first date for the group.
The fact that the presence or absence of fusae can help date a composition
supports my earlier contention that the presence or absence of semiminims
is a chronological matter. There is no reason to suspect that any of the
pieces in Group 9 were written before this date, nor that any works in my
earlier groups were written after it—with the exception of the three works
in Group 8[b]. The only quarrel with the date is that it might not be quite
accurate, but it is undoubtedly in the proper decade.

---

[1] Houday, Histoire artistique, p. 195.

[2] Ibid., p. 195.

[3] J. Marix, Histoire de la musique et des musiciens de la cour de Bourgogne (Strasbourg, 1939), p. 39.

What might be called Dufay's classical style of mensural practice
prevails in the works of this group. O and ₵ are used as initial signatures, with the cipher 3 often appearing in the course of sections in ₵.
Coloration is used frequently under ₵, and in every case there is a clear
distinction between it and (₵)3, even though the two are used interchange-
ably by certain other composers. Assuming that O is transcribed into
modern notation as 3/4, with the semibreve becoming a quarter note, ₵
should be 2/2, with the breve a half note, and passages in (₵)3 should be
left in the same meter, with quarter-note triplets.

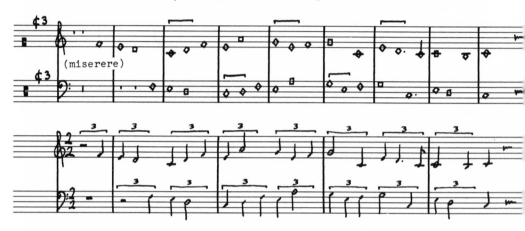

Musical Example 46: Dufay, <u>Missa</u> <u>ecce</u> <u>ancilla</u> (Agnus Dei II)

Sections in coloration under ₵ move in what should be transcribed as 3/2,
with a quarter note of this meter equaling a quarter note of the transcription of (₵)3.

Musical Example 47: Dufay, <u>Missa</u> <u>ecce</u> <u>ancilla</u> (Patrem)

Thus there is a basic difference between the two: coloration under C has become breve coloration, while the cipher 3 in (C)3 operates at the semi-breve level.

Movement in O is in semibreves and minims, with semiminims more numerous than breves and with a sprinkling of fusae. A count of movement in the first section of the Missa ave regina gives:

		longs	breves	semibreves	minims	semiminims	fusae
Kyrie	O	6	24	128	124	32	1
Christe	C	10	118	146	94	14	-

Here, movement in C is in breves, semibreves and minims, with the number of breves roughly equal to minims, and with some semiminims but no fusae in this mensuration. In general, then, movement in the two most common mensurations tends toward smaller notes than had been used in earlier works, suggesting either that the beat was slowing down, as Besseler would have it, or that composers wanted "busier" music, with more notes in a given time.

Movement in smaller notes in C is even more marked in the few secular works written in this mensuration, so much so that it becomes semi-breve-minim movement. A count of the superius and contra of Vostre bruit shows this:

	longs	breves	semibreves	minims	semiminims	fusae
C	3	7	89	125	31	2

In the previous chapter I put three works in a sub-group, 8^b, on the basis of their abnormal (for Group 8) movement in C, in semibreves and minims. I suggested that they must date from a later period than the other works in Group 8, and it seems clear enough that they belong chronologically in my Group 9, kept from it only by the accident of not having fusae.

C has disappeared for all practical purposes. It is used only in Les doleurs, a tour de force with conflicting signatures combined with a canon, in one section of the Missa l'homme arme in which Dufay amuses him-self by using archaic mensurations, and, exceptionally, as an initial sig-nature in Helas mon dueil, a piece which has come down to us in only one manuscript, Porto.

Dissonance invariably lasted for the duration of a minim in O and a semibreve in C in the compositions of Groups 6, 7 and 8. This is still true of the sacred pieces of Group 9, in general, but a few interior cadences in C have suspended dissonance holding for only a minim. And in the few secular works using C, such dissonance regularly lasts for a minim. (See Ex. 48.)

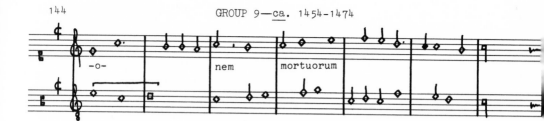

Musical Example 48: Dufay, <u>Missa</u> <u>ave</u> <u>regina</u> (Patrem, SPB80 18'19)

   The first theorists to speak of the speed of the beat, men of the
generation of Ramos, were writing in the last three decades of the century.
I was reluctant to apply what they had to say to the early Dufay works because of the gap of almost half a century between these compositions and
such theoretical writings. But the works of Group 9 are almost contemporary with these treatises, and since theorists were in almost complete
agreement that the semibreve in "normal" mensurations went along at a
speed equivalent to the rate of the human pulse, we can say that sections
in tempus perfectum in the late Dufay works moved at approximately seventy
semibreves per minute. In a transcription in 3/4, the tempo is M.M. = 70.
Equating a semibreve of O with a breve of ₵, we can say that ₵ went at
a rate of seventy breves, or one hundred and forty semibreves, per minute,
and (₵)3 moved at seventy breves, or two hundred and ten semibreves, per
minute.

   The <u>Missa</u> <u>l'homme</u> <u>arme</u> fits in my Group 9, supporting Besseler's
contention that this work was written after the tenor masses <u>Se</u> <u>la</u> <u>face</u>
and <u>Caput</u>, which fall in my Group 8. In one curious passage in the <u>Missa</u>
<u>l'homme</u> <u>arme</u> several signatures are introduced which the composer had not
used for some decades.

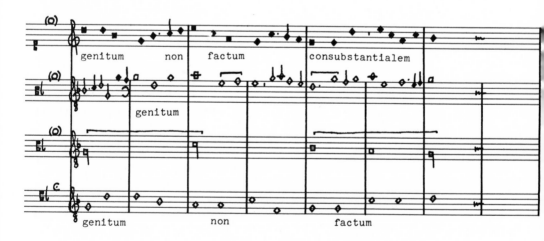

Musical Example 49: Dufay, <u>Missa</u> <u>l'homme</u> <u>arme</u> (Patrem)

All voices have been moving along calmly in tempus perfectum; suddenly, the almost obsolete signature C appears in the lowest voice, used as Dufay had used it in his youth, with minim equivalence between it and tempus perfectum. One breve later, the contra has the signature Ɔ, which Dufay had not used since he abandoned major prolation around 1430. There is no precedent for his use of this signature in relation to O; in works of the 1420's and 1430's he had used it only with C or Φ. It had always brought about a 4:3 relationship, however, and here it causes a long of two breves (each of the two semibreves) replace a breve of three semibreves, i.e., four semibreves to replace three. The most curious voice in this passage, though, is the superius, in which coloration is introduced in O. In every other piece in this mensuration with coloration, we have either minim coloration, with three colored minims replacing two normal ones, or breve coloration, again with three colored breves replacing two; the semibreve remains the constant factor in both, being equivalent in coloration to what it is in normal use. But here we find nine colored semibreves replacing six normal ones. This is wholly without precedent in the Dufay works, and I can only conjecture that Dufay indicated this abnormal relationship by some signature not preserved in the present source.

    Coloration under (¢)3 is also common in the works of this group, curiously bringing about the same 3/2 feeling resulting from coloration under ¢.

Musical Example 50: Dufay, _Missa ecce ancilla_ (Agnus Dei II)

    In his last works, Dufay completes a cycle in his mensural practice. Three basic mensurations were used in his earliest pieces, C, O, and C; from the mid-1420's until the 1440's or 1450's, he used a much greater variety of signatures and mensurations; and he returned, in the works of the last decades of his life, to the use of three basic mensurations, now O, ¢, and (¢)3. Two of the basic mensurations in both his early and late works were organized as "triple" time, the other as duple:

Early: $\mathbb{C}$ 2, 2, 3   Late: O   2, 3, 2
        C   2, 2, 2 $\mathbb{C}$ 2, 2, 2
        O   2, 3, 2   ($\mathbb{C}$)3 2, 3, 2

Assuming a beat on the minim in $\mathbb{C}$ and on the semibreve in O, the two are
equivalent, the only difference being one of tempo; if the beat remained
on the semibreve in O in the later works, this mensuration can be matched
with $\mathbb{C}$ and O of the early group. Assuming a beat on the semibreve in C
in the first group and on the breve in $\mathbb{C}$ in the second, these two are com-
parable. But if we assume a beat on the breve in ($\mathbb{C}$)3 in the last works,
we can find no matching mensuration in the early group.

        The problem of the scarcity of late Dufay works becomes even more
acute with this last group. If my chronological groupings are accurate,
only three masses, one motet, and a handful of secular works date from the
last two and a half decades of his life, of the more than two hundred works
attributed to him. One would think that he wrote more than this; judging
from the excellence of those works known to have been written at this time,
he was in full possession of his faculties. In addition, the archives at
Cambrai record the copying of certain Dufay works which have not been preserved. Lip service was paid to him long after his death, and theorists
continued to refer to him and his compositions; but the works themselves
went out of fashion, and it is exceptional to find one of them in a manuscript copied more than a decade after his death. It is unfortunate that
his works were not copied into the magnificent Flemish manuscripts of the
very end of the century and the beginning of the next.

        It is quite likely, then, that Dufay wrote more music in the last
decades of his life than is attributed to him. Feininger has suggested
that a number of anonymous masses and mass fragments of the period are by
Dufay,[4] and I have put four of these which most conform to the composer's
mensural usage in Group 9[a]. Certainly one basis of Feininger's attribution of these works to Dufay was their obvious resemblance to the late
Dufay masses on several superficial levels: all are tenor masses and all
have motto beginnings for all four voices. It should be said in his de-
fense that there are not many masses by composers other than Dufay which
do this. From the point of view of mensural usage, three of them—Missa
Christus surrexit, Missa veterem hominem, and Missa puisque je vis—agree
with Dufay's practices, and here also it must be pointed out that it is
not easy to find works by other composers which do not deviate in some way
from this. It may not be possible to prove, at least at this point in the
development of the science of musicology, that these works are by Dufay,

---

[4] Feininger, Monumenta, Series I, Tomus II, pp. 1-4.

but I find their attribution to him more convincing than Feininger's attribution of the eleven cycles of propers.

Besseler accepts only one of these, the Missa la mort de Saint Gothard, which he says "in every detail so much reflects Dufay's advanced style, and moreover...is of such a high artistic value, that, in the light of our present knowledge, no other musician of about 1450 but Dufay can be honored as its author."[5] Curiously, this is the only one of Feininger's group showing deviations from Dufay's normal mensural practice. The mensurations O and ₵ are used, there is a passage in (₵)3, and fusae are used; so it belongs with the other works. But movement in both O and ₵ is in semibreves and minims:

		longs	breves	semibreves	minims	semiminims
Kyrie	O	1	-	49	53	19
Kyrie	₵	2	-	34	38	11

Semibreve-minim movement is found in no other Dufay mass (or motet) under ₵. Furthermore, suspended dissonance is held for a minim in both O and ₵ in this mass, and in other sacred works of the period attributed to Dufay dissonance holds for a semibreve in ₵, with few exceptions. Fusae are found here in sections in ₵, and in no other Dufay sacred work can notes of this value be found under this signature. The "Et incarnatus" section of the Credo has a signature of C2 in the superius against, and equivalent to, ₵ in the other voices; this signature is found in no authentic Dufay work. Other features of the mass are atypical of Dufay: an O ₵ ₵ pattern is used for the Kyrie and Agnus Dei; and c.o.p. ligatures, which in late Dufay invariably begin on the first semibreve of the "measure," i.e., on the first of the three semibreves making up a breve, here commence at other points.

The Missa Christus surrexit, the Missa verterem hominem, and the Missa puisque je vis, on the other hand, use only O, ₵, and (₵)3, with semibreve-minim movement and a few fusae under O and breve-semibreve (-minim) movement with no fusae under ₵. Dissonance is allowed on the minim in O and on the semibreve in ₵. The masses may not be by Dufay, but their attribution to him cannot be questioned on the basis of mensural usage. The Missa veterem hominem, incidentally, is remarkably similar to the Missa caput: both are constructed on a bipartite pattern; both use a portion of a chant from the Sarum rite as a cantus; both break this into several sections whose length is kept invariable throughout the mass, though the fragments are introduced by, and separated by, free sections of variable length. The scheme of this mass is:

---

[5] Besseler, Opera Omnia, III, p. ii.

		A		B		C			D		E
Kyrie	O̲	(19)	24	(20)	8	(1)	25	₵	(36)	36	(16)	48
Et in terra	O̲	(16)	24	(8)	8	(1)	25	₵	(30)	36	(10)	48
Patrem	O̲	(16)	24	(8)	8	(1)	25	₵	(32)	36	(12)	48
Sanctus	O̲	(18)	24	(8)	8	(11)	25	₵	(48)	36	(12)	48
Agnus Dei	O̲	(16)	24	(10)	8	(11)	25	₵	(24)	36	(8)	48

Morley, in the course of a discussion of whether major and minor mode in tempus perfectum should be major or minor, prints a fragment of this mass in black notation, offering it as "one example which was made before any of the aforenamed [Dr. Fayrfax, Dr. Newton, Dr. Cooper, Dr. Kirbye, Dr. Tye, etc.] were born."[6] The use of the Sarum version of chant, the fact that the "English figure" is used repeatedly, and this mention by Morley all suggest that the Missa veterem hominem is an English work. But the first two arguments could be raised against accepting the Dufay Missa caput as anything but an English work, and Morley's quotation of a portion of the former mass in black notation from what must have been an English manuscript is matched by the fact that a portion of the Missa caput has been found, in black notation, in what must be an English manuscript. The layout of the tenor of the Missa veterem hominem is strikingly similar to that of the Missa caput, more so than to other English masses of this period, which tend to have an invariable number of rests between fragments of the cantus firmus as in the Leonel Power Missa alma redemptoris.

If it is ever possible to transfer the masses of Group 9[a] to Group 9 and to detect other Dufay masses, motets, and other works among the anonymous works with which manuscripts of the period abound, the number of late Dufay compositions will be brought more in line with what might be expected.

---

[9] Morley, A Plain and Easy Introduction, Harman edition, p. 124. Thurston Dart identified this composition in "A Footnote for Morley's 'Plain and Easy Introduction,'" M&L, 35 (1954), p. 183

THE WORKS OF GROUP 9
ca. 1454-1474

Distinguishing characteristics: use of fusae.

Missa ave regina celorum
    Kyrie   O ¢ 3 O
    Et in terra   O ¢ 3 ¢
    Patrem   O ¢ 3 ¢   Missa l'homme arme
    Sanctus   O ¢   Kyrie   O ¢ O
    Agnus Dei   O ¢ ¢   Et in terra   O ¢
                         Patrem

Missa ecce ancilla Domini   superius: O   ¢ 3 ¢
    Kyrie   O ¢ O   motetus: O Ɔ O ¢
    Et in terra   O ¢   contra: O   ¢
    Patrem   O ¢   tenor: O Ꞓ O ¢ 3 ¢
    Sanctus   O ¢   Sanctus   O ¢ 3 C O
    Agnus Dei   O ¢ 3 O   Agnus Dei   O ¢ O

Ave regina celorum
O ¢ 3 C

Exultet celum (contratenor by Dufay)
O

De ma haulte   Je triumph de crudel dueil
O   (O)

Du tout m'estoie   Le serviteur
¢   O

Franc cueur gentile   Les doleurs
(O)   (C)/(O)

Helas mon dueil   Malheureulx cueur
C   O ¢

Je ne vis oncques   Mon seul plaisir
O   O

149

Resistera   Vostre bruit
O   ¢

THE WORKS OF GROUP 9^a
(anonymous masses attributed to Dufay)

Missa Christus surrexit   Missa la mort de Saint Gothard
   Et in terra   O ¢ 3 ¢   Kyrie   O ¢ ¢
   Patrem   O ¢   Et in terra   O ¢ O
   Sanctus   O 3 O ¢   Patrem   O C 2/¢ 3 O
                                  Sanctus   O ¢ O
                                  Agnus Dei   O ¢ ¢

Missa puisque je vis   Missa veterem hominem
   Kyrie   O ¢ O   Kyrie   O ¢
   Et in terra   O ¢   Et in terra   O ¢
   Patrem   O ¢   Patrem   O ¢
   Sanctus   O ¢ 3   Sanctus   O ¢
   Agnus Dei   O ¢   Agnus Dei   O ¢

SUMMARY, CONCLUSIONS, PROPOSALS

I have divided the Dufay works into nine groups, each clearly
differentiated from all others by details of mensural usage, and I
have suggested dates for each group on the basis of datable works
within each, and other evidence. The defining dates of the various
groups are by no means mutually exclusive, but overlap. A summary
of the characteristics of each group follows.

151

GROUP 1 (ca. 1415-1423)

Distinguishing characteristics: use of ¢, C and O as basic mensurations; semibreve-minim movement in each; no semiminims.

signatures	organization	movement	coloration	remarks
Initial				
¢	2,2,3	semibreve-minim	semibreve	–
O	2,3,2	semibreve-minim	minim, breve	–
C	2,2,2	semibreve-minim	minim, semibreve	semibreve coloration exceptional, found in only one piece
⊙	2,3,3	semibreve-minim	–	exceptional, found only once
Interior				
(O)2	3,2,2	semibreve-minim	–	O semibreve = (O)2 breve
(O)3	2,3,3	semibreve-minim	–	O semibreve = (O)3 semibreve
(¢)2	2,3,2	semibreve-minim	–	¢ minim = (¢)2 semibreve
(¢)3	2,3,3	semibreve-minim	–	(¢)2 semibreve = (¢2)3 semibreve

GROUP 2 (1423-1429)

Distinguishing characteristics: use of ₵, C, and O as basic mensurations; semibreve-minim movement in ₵ but a shift to breve-semibreve movement in O and C; flagged semiminims in O and C, and either no semiminims or a scattering of flagged semiminims in O and C.

signatures	organization	movement	coloration	remarks
Initial				
₵	2,2,3	semibreve-minim	semibreve	-
O	2,3,2	breve-semibreve	minim, breve	-
C	2,2,2	breve-semibreve	minim	-
Interior				
(₵)2	2,3,2	semibreve-minim	-	₵ minim = (₵)2 semibreve
(O)3	2,3,3	semibreve-minim	-	O semibreve = (O)3 semibreve
Ɔ	2,2,2	breve-semibreve-minim	-	₵ semibreve = Ɔ breve

GROUP 2^a (ca. 1415-1429)

Distinguishing characteristics: use of ₵ with flagged semiminims; semibreve-minim movement.

signatures	organization	movement	coloration	remarks
Initial				
₵	2,2,3	semibreve-minim	semibreve	-
Interior				
(₵)2	2,3,2	semibreve, minim	-	-

GROUP 2^b (1423-1433)

Distinguishing characteristics: use of O or C; breve-semibreve movement; no semiminims, or a scattering of flagged semiminims.

signatures	organization	movement	coloration	remarks
Initial				
O	2,3,2	breve-semibreve	breve	-
C	2,2,2	breve-semibreve	-	-

Distinguishing characteristics: use of both C and φ; flagged semiminims.

GROUP 3 (1426-1431)

signatures Initial	organization	movement	coloration	remarks
C	2,2,3	semibreve-minim	semibreve	–
O	2,3,2	(breve)-semibreve-minim	minim, breve	–
C	2,2,2	(breve)-semibreve-minim	–	–
φ	2,3,2	(breve)-semibreve-minim	breve	–
⊙	2,3,3	–	–	used only in tenor
¢	2,2,3	–	–	used only in tenor
¢	2,2,2	breve-semibreve	semibreve, breve	used only one piece, which may not belong in this group
¢3	2,3,2	breve-semibreve	–	used only one piece, which may not belong in this group
φ	2,3,3	semibreve-minim	–	exceptional, used in only one piece
Interior				
C	2,2,2	(breve)-semibreve-minim	–	φ breve - C long

GROUP 4 (1426-1433)

Distinguishing characteristics: use of φ with flagged semiminims.

signature	organization	movement	coloration	remarks
Initial				
O	2,3,2	semibreve-minim	breve	--
φ	2,3,2	semibreve-minim	breve	--
₵3	2,3,2	semibreve-minim	breve	used only in tenor
⊙	2,3,3	--	--	
Interior				
(O)3	2,3,3	semibreve-minim	--	O semibreve = (O)3 semi-breve
C	2,2,2	breve-semibreve	--	φ breve = C long

GROUP 5 (1433-1435)

Distinguishing characteristics: liturgical pieces notated in pseudo-score; alternation of chant and polyphony; chant paraphrase in superius; colored semiminims.

signature	organization	movement	coloration	remarks
Initial				
O	2,3,2	semibreve-minim	minim, breve	--
φ	2,3,2	semibreve-minim	breve	--
C	2,2,2	semibreve-minim	--	used in only two works
₵	2,2,2	breve-semibreve	--	used in only one work
Ɔ	2,2,3	semibreve-minim	semibreve	used in only one work
Interior				
(O)3	2,3,3	semibreve-minim	semibreve	O semibreve = (O)3 semi-breve

GROUP 6 (1433-ca. 1445)

Distinguishing characteristics: use of Φ with colored semiminims.

signatures	organization	movement	coloration	remarks
Initial				
O	2,3,2	semibreve-minim	breve	–
Φ	2,3,2	semibreve-minim	breve	–
C	2,2,2	semibreve-minim	minim	–
¢ (= C)	2,2,2	breve-semibreve	semibreve	–
₵	2,2,3	semibreve-minim	–	used in only one piece
Interior				
(Φ)3	2,3,2	breve-semibreve	breve	Φ breve = (Φ)3 breve
(O)3	2,3,3	semibreve-minim	minim	O semibreve = (O)3 semibreve
$(\Phi 3)_4$	2,2,2	breve-semibreve	breve	(Φ)3 breve = $(\Phi 3)_4$ long
$(C)_4^6$	2,3,2	semibreve-minim	–	used in only one work; C breve = $(C)_4^6$ breve

GROUP 7 (1433-ca. 1455)

Distinguishing characteristics: use of tempus perfectum only; colored semiminims and no fusae.

signatures	organization	movement	coloration	remarks
Initial				
O	2,3,2	semibreve-minim	minim, breve	suspended dissonance on semibreve

GROUP 8 (1435-ca. 1460)

Distinguishing characteristics: use of O and ¢ (with breve-semibreve movement) as basic mensurations; colored semiminims and no fusae.

Initial

signatures	organization	movement	coloration	remarks
O	2,3,2	semibreve-minim	minim, breve	suspended dissonance on minim
¢ (=C)	2,2,2	breve-semibreve	minim, breve	suspended dissonance on semibreve
¢3 (=C3)	2,3,2	breve – semibreve	breve	suspended dissonance on semibreve

Interior

signatures				
(¢)3 (=C3)	identical with ¢3 as an initial signature			

GROUP 8ᵃ (1435-ca. 1445)

Distinguishing characteristics: use of O and C (with semibreve-minim movement) as basic mensurations; colored semiminims and no fusae.

Initial

signatures	organization	movement	coloration	remarks
O	2,3,2	semibreve-minim	minim, breve	suspended dissonance on minim
C	2,2,2	semibreve-minim	minim, semibreve	

GROUP 8^b (ca. 1454-1474)

Distinguishing characteristics: use of ¢ with semibreve-minim movement; colored semibreves and no fusae.

signatures	organization	movement	coloration	remarks
Initial				
O	2,3,2	semibreve-minim	minim, breve	—
¢	2,2,2	semibreve-minim	minim, semibreve	suspended dissonance on minim
Interior				
(¢)3	2,3,2	breve-semibreve	breve	¢ breve = (¢)3 breve

GROUP 9 (ca. 1454-1474)

Distinguishing characteristics: use of fusae.

signatures	organization	movement	coloration	remarks
Initial				
O	2,3,2	semibreve-minim	minim, breve	suspended dissonance on minim
¢	2,2,2	breve-semibreve-minim	minim, breve	suspended dissonance on semibreve, sometimes on minim in secular pieces used in only three pieces, may be mistake for ¢
C (= ¢?)	2,2,2	semibreve-minim	minim	
Interior				
(¢)3	2,3,2	breve-semibreve	breve	¢ breve = (¢)3 breve
ꞓ	2,2,3	semibreve-minim	—	O minim = ꞓ minim; found in only one piece
Ɔ	2,2,2	breve-semibreve	—	O breve = Ɔ long; found in only one piece

This study has been based on the assumption that Dufay used the same signatures to mean the same things throughout his life, and that changes in his mensural practice consisted of the addition and subtraction of certain mensurations from time to time and in variation of movement under some signatures from one period to another. I have suggested approximate dates of composition for all Dufay works which cannot be dated from external evidence and raised the possibility that certain pieces attributed to him may be by other composers because of their deviation from his normal mensural usage. I have also suggested that several anonymous works might be by Dufay, since they adhere so closely to his mensural practice.

The criteria which I have used to date the Dufay works should also be useable to date compositions by such men as Binchois and Regis, who were in close contact with Dufay and his music

From time to time in this study I have pointed out differences between Dufay's mensural practice and that of other composers. I have selected, virtually at random, two other pieces written in the late fifteenth century and propose to examine their mensural usage to demonstrate a final time how clearly differences in practice from one composer to another show up in such an examination. The first piece is the Ockeghem Missa quinti toni, a three-voice mass preserved in the Chigi manuscript and in Br5557. This is probably an early work, perhaps contemporary with the masses of Dufay in Group 9; thus, differences between this work and Dufay are differences of personal style, not chronological ones. The general mensuration scheme of this mass is:

Kyrie	C	C	C
Et in terra	C	¢	
Patrem	C	C	¢
Sanctus	C	C	¢ ¢
Agnus Dei	C	C	C

Just this much tells us that the piece could not possibly be by Dufay, for there is a complete absence of any sort of triple time. He contrasted tempus perfectum and tempus imperfectum in every one of his extended works after 1433-1435—masses, motets, and even the longer secular works. The only coloration in the Ockeghem mass is minim coloration,[1] and there are no interior signatures to bring about even temporary changes to triple organization.

Another difference is that dissonance regularly falls on the minim in both C and ¢ in the Ockeghem (though in a few instances it falls on the semibreve in the latter mensuration). In the Dufay masses and motets,

---

[1] Or minor color, which at this time is interchangeable with the pattern dotted minim—semiminim, the same piece often having one form of the figure in one manuscript and the other in another.

suspended dissonance regularly lasts for the duration of a minim in O and
C and a semibreve in ¢. A count of movement in the Et in terra of the
Ockeghem reveals a slight difference in movement between C and ¢:

	longs	breves	semibreves	minims	semiminims	fusae
C	1	6	48	144	31	8
¢	1	11	88	75	26	2

Movement under C is in semibreves and minims, as in Dufay, but it approaches
minim-semiminim movement, which does not happen in the few late Dufay works
using this signature. There is also semibreve-minim movement under ¢, with
semiminims outnumbering breves by a considerable margin, while ¢ moves in
breves and semibreves in the Dufay masses. Fusae are never found under ¢
in the Dufay sacred works, but there are several in this Ockeghem mass.

C and ¢ were clearly not thought of as being in a 2:1 ratio to
one another in this Ockeghem mass, since movement under both is in semibreves
and minims and suspended dissonance falls on the minim in both. The line
through the C in ¢ is not a sign of proportion, but a tempo indication.

The deviations from Dufay's mensural practice can be seen at a
glance. And another glance, this one at the Ockeghem Requiem Mass which
follows the Missa quinti toni in Chigi, shows us that there is change in this
composer's practice also: the very first section of the Requiem Mass has a
section in ¢ with breve-semibreve movement, with dissonance regularly falling on the semibreve. Variations in practice of this sort in the Dufay works
were explainable as chronological changes, and it is quite possible that a
detailed study of mensural usage in the Ockeghem works would yield similar
results.

The second work, the Josquin Missa l'homme arme super voces musicales, is a much more complex, and probably later, piece than the Ockeghem.
The first section has the mensuration pattern:

Kyrie   O   (tenor: ⊙)

Christe ¢   (tenor: C)

Kyrie   φ   (tenor: ⊙)

Movement in O, ¢, and φ is in minims and semiminims, with semiminims outnumbering semibreves in each. Dissonance is allowed on the minim in each of
the three, though on occasion it lasts for only a semiminim.

Josquin follows the convention of having major prolation imply
augmentation—when it is used in the tenor. A transcription of the two
Kyries reveals that a minim of ⊙ equals a semibreve of O, and that a minim
of ⊙ also equals a semibreve of φ. O and φ are both organized with
three semibreves to the breve and two minims to the semibreve, as in Dufay,
and the difference between the two can only be one of tempo. Thus we have
another piece, this one probably written within a decade or two of the

beginning of the sixteenth century, in which the theory of a tactus of invariable speed cannot be sustained.

We see from a transcription of the Christe that a breve of ₵
equals a minim of ₡, and again invoking the principle that two things each
equal to a third must be equal to one another, a breve of ₵ equals a semibreve of O, each being equal to a minim of ₡ or ⊙. The relationship between ₵ and ₡ is made explicit in the Petrucci print of the mass: the superius has the cantus firmus, in major prolation, in the third Agnus Dei,
and the singer of this part has been furnished a resolutio in ₵ in which
minims in ₡ are rewritten as breves in ₵.

There is a change in the late Dufay works from breve-semibreve
movement in ₵ to semibreve-minim movement in O, and suspended dissonance
is allowed on one note in ₵ (semibreve) but on another in O (minim). In
this Josquin mass there is minim-semiminim movement under both O and ₵
and dissonance lasts for a minim in each; if the tactus went at a constant
rate of speed, falling on the semibreve in O and the breve in ₵, sections
in the latter mensuration would go twice as fast as those in O. This seems
improbable; it is more likely that if the beat were on the breve in ₵, this
beat was markedly slower than the beat on the semibreve in O. Thus, in
this first section of the Missa l'homme armé, far from finding a tactus
moving at a constant rate of speed in all mensurations, we see that the beat
must go at a different pace in each of the three primary mensurations:

O moderate, on the semibreve
Φ faster than moderate, on the semibreve
₵ slower than moderate, on the breve

The mensuration schemes of the next two sections are:

Et in terra   O   (tenor: ⊙ ₡ ⊙)
Qui tollis   ₵   (tenor: ⊙ ₡ ⊙)

Patrem   O   (tenor: ⊙ ₡ ⊙)
Et incarnatus   ₵   (tenor: ⊙ ₡ ⊙)
Confiteor   ₵   (tenor: ⊙ ₡ ⊙)

Relationships between the various mensurations are the same as in the Kyrie.
The tenor is marked "equivalet" in the "Confiteor" section, the effect of
this direction being to replace breve-minim equivalence between ₵ and ⊙
by temporary minim equivalence. There is no difficulty in transcription,
but a curious situation arises in performance: if the beat is on the breve
in ₵, as I have assumed, four minims grouped as two semibreves of two minims
each fall under each beat. But since there is minim equivalence in this
passage, four minims of ⊙ also fall under each beat, and since minims are
grouped by threes in this mensuration, the first note of a group of three
minims is sung on the beat only once every third beat—or a Grosstakt of
three beats is set up between the two mensurations.

The Sanctus begins conventionally enough in tempus perfectum, but
soon there are even more differences between Josquin's mensural practice
and that of Dufay. The "Pleni sunt" section is in C, the first time this
signature has appeared in the mass, and movement is in semiminims and fusae
with suspended dissonance on the semiminim. C thus appears to be in proportion to ¢, in which there is minim-semiminim movement and dissonance on
the minim. The curious thing here is that if we assume C to be the "integer valor," then we must assume that normal movement in this mass is in
semiminims and fusae; ¢ would then be in duple proportion to C, clearly
enough, but so would O. In this mass, Josquin seems to have thought of O
and ¢ as his "normal" mensurations, with C in augmentation.

Josquin uses the signature C3 in the "Osanna" section to mean
just what it did in the Dufay works and just what the tact-tables never say
it to mean: three minims replace two, the resulting mensuration having two
semibreves to the breve and three minims to the semibreve. This organization is the same as that of ₵, the difference between the two being one of
tempo, with the beat on the minim in ₵ but on the semibreve in C3.
Strangely, the two are used against one another in this section, the tenor
having ₵ against C3 in the other voices, and from a transcription we see
that there is minim equivalence between the two, which seems to disprove my
explanation of the difference between them. But the tenor has the canon
"Gaudet cum gaudentibus," and the meaning of this hitherto obscure direction
is now clear: the tenors are instructed to rejoice <u>along</u> <u>with</u> the other
voices, i.e., to sing three minims to the beat, as the others are doing,
rather than to sing one minim to the beat as they have been doing in the
mensuration up to this point.

The "Benedictus" is made up of three two-in-one canons, for two
bass, two altus, and two superius voices, and the signatures C and ¢ are
used in the Petrucci print in each of the three duets to indicate a duple
proportion between the two voices. Heyden, however, in the course of an
explanation of the various ways in which diminution can be indicated,
quotes these three duets as illustrations of three different methods.[2]
Diminution may be indicated by the use of the cipher 2, he says, quoting
the superius duet with signatures of C and C2; a virgula through a signature brings about the same result, he continues, quoting the altus duet
with the signatures C and ¢; the third method is to invert a signature,
he says, quoting the bass duet with signatures of C and Ɔ . There seems
little question that Heyden has altered Josquin's original signatures for
didactic purposes, though.

---

[2] S. Heyden, <u>De</u> <u>arte</u> <u>canendi</u>, pp. 103-104.

The scheme for the Agnus Dei is:

Agnus Dei O   (tenor: ⊙ ₵)
Agnus Dei C/ ₵/ ₵3 (a three-in-one canon)
Agnus Dei ₵   (superius: ⊙)

The only new signature is ₵3, calling for an organization of three semi-breves to the breve and two minims to the semibreve, as in Dufay. The men-surations used in the mass, then, are:

signatures	organization	movement	beat
O	2,3,2	minim-semiminim	semibreve
₵	2,2,2	minim-semiminim	breve
Φ	2,3,2	minim-semiminim	semibreve
C3	2,2,3	minim-semiminim	semibreve
C	2,2,2	semiminim-fusae	semibreve
ℂ	2,2,3	(used in tenor)	minim
⊙	2,3,3	(used in tenor)	minim
₵3	2,3,2	(used in canon)	breve

It takes no more than a glance at this piece to see the numerous deviations from Dufay's mensural practice—and also the deviations from Ockeghem's practice.

I have no doubt that detailed studies of the works of other com-posers of the fifteenth century, and probably other centuries as well, would reveal chronological changes in their mensural usage and differences between their practice and that of other composers which could be useful tools to help solve problems of chronology and authenticity, just as they have for Dufay.

APPENDIX A

THE DUFAY WORKS

<u>MASSES</u>

Group

<u>Missa</u> <u>ave</u> <u>regina</u> <u>celorum</u>   9
   Br5557 110'120'; SPB80 9'20'; ModE, mass no. xiv

<u>Missa</u> <u>caput</u>   8[a]
   Tr89 246'256
  Kyrie: Tr88 31'33
  Et in terra: Tr90 96'98; Tr93 126'128
  Patrem: Tr90 168'170; Tr93 236'238
  Sanctus: Tr90 228'230; Tr93 297'299
  Agnus Dei: Tr88 33'35; Cov 1-1'

<u>Missa</u> <u>ecce</u> <u>ancilla</u> <u>Domini</u>   9
   Br5557 50'61; RS 14 76'86

<u>Missa</u> <u>l'homme</u> <u>arme</u>   9
  RS 49 36'55; Sc 26'42
  Kyrie, Et in terra: RS 14 101'105

<u>Missa</u> <u>Sancti</u> <u>Jacobi</u>   3
  BL 144-152[b]
  Kyrie: Ao 20'21'; Ao 50'52; Tr87 1-2; Tr90 67'70;
    Tr93 100'101
  Et in terra: Ao 64'65'
  Patrem: Ao 119'122; Tr87 151'153'; Tr92 118'120
  Sanctus: Ao 149'150
  Agnus Dei: Ao 154'155
  Communio: Tr87 57

<u>Missa</u> <u>se</u> <u>la</u> <u>face</u>   8[b]
   Tr88 97'106; RS 14 27'38

Missa sine nomine   1
   BL 10-16
   Kyrie: BU 9; Ven 1'2; Ao 26'27; Ao 49'50
   Et in terra: Ao 32'33; Ao 67'68; Ao 71'67; Ven 3'5;
         Tr90 165'166; Tr92 125'126; Tr93 197'198
   Patrem: BU 32-33; Ven 22'25; Ao 33'34; Ao 129'132
   Sanctus: Ven 9'11; Ao 151'152
   Agnus Dei: Ven 11'12; Ao 155'156

                   Masses of Questionable Authenticity

Missa Sancti Anthonii   6
   Tr90 72'73; 395'406
   Kyrie: Tr93 103'104

                 Anonymous Masses Attributed to Dufay

Missa Christus surrexit   9[a]
   Tr89 342'349

Missa la mort de Saint Gothard   9[a]
   ModE, mass no. ii(14'25)

Missa puisque je vis   9[a]
   RS 14 160'170

Missa veterem hominem   9[a]
   Tr88 1'9, 264'266

                            PARTIAL MASSES

Kyrie (BL 17; Ao 24)   1
Sanctus qui ianuas mortis (BL 21)
Agnus Dei (BL 23)

Kyrie (BL 187; Ven 2'; Ao 25'; Ao 49; MuEm 31;   1
      Ca6 2; Ca11 2)
Et in terra (BL 187[b]; Ao 94'95)
Patrem (BL 188; Ao 102'104)

Et in terra (BL 35-36; Ao 60'62; MuEm 40'41'; Ca6 2'5;   1
      Ca11 6'8)
Patrem (BL 37-39; BU 52-55; Ao 126'129; Ca6 5'10; Ca11 23'27)

Et in terra (BL 138-139; Ao 96'98; Tr87 10'12; Tr92 13'15;   2
      Ca6 10'13; Ca11 11'13)

<u>Patrem</u> (BL 140-142; Ao 108'111; Tr87 12'15; Tr90 190'193;
        Tr92 15'16; Tr93 260'263; Ca6 13'17; Ca11 27'31)

<u>Et</u> <u>in</u> <u>terra</u> (BL 40; Ox 60'61; Ao 30'31; Tr90 141'142; Tr93 171'172)   1
<u>Patrem</u> (BL 41-42; Ao 30'32; Ao 104'106; MuEm 42'43; Tr87 249'251;
        Tr90 200-202; Tr93 234'; Tr93 270-272)

<u>Sanctus</u> (Tr92 216-217)   6
<u>Agnus</u> <u>Dei</u> (Tr92 217'218)

<u>Sanctus</u> (BL 133; Tr92 6'7'; Tr92 218'219')   6
<u>Agnus</u> <u>Dei</u> (BL 134; Tr92 219'220)

<u>Sanctus</u> <u>papale</u> (BL 135-137; Tr90 277-279'; Tr92 213'215;   6
        Tr93 350-352')
<u>Agnus</u> <u>Dei</u> <u>custos</u> <u>et</u> <u>pastor</u> (Tr92 208'210)

INDIVIDUAL MASS SECTIONS

<u>Kyrie</u>   8
    Tr90 90'91; Tr92 144; Tr93 122'123; Ca6 4'6; Ca11 2'3

<u>Kyrie</u> <u>cum</u> <u>iubilo</u>   5
    BL 124^b; MuEm 57; Tr90 85; Tr92 64'; Tr93 117

<u>Kyrie</u> <u>cunctipotens</u> <u>genitor</u>   5
    BL 157^b; BU 83; MuEm 31'32; Ao 22; Tr92 27; Tr93

<u>Kyrie</u> <u>de</u> <u>apostolis</u>   5
    Tr87 93'; Tr87 101'102; MuEm 102'103

<u>Kyrie</u> <u>de</u> <u>martyribus</u> (= in diebus Dominicis)   5
    Ao 27'28; MuEm 33'34; Tr87 94; Tr90 81'82; Tr92 38';
        Tr93 112'113

<u>Kyrie</u> <u>fons</u> <u>bonitatis</u>   5
    BL 127; MuEm 127'128; Tr90 64'65; Tr93 93'94

<u>Kyrie</u> <u>in</u> <u>Dominicis</u> <u>diebus</u>   7
    BL 126

<u>Kyrie</u> <u>in</u> <u>semiduplicibus</u> <u>maioribus</u>   7
    BL 128

<u>Kyrie</u> <u>in</u> <u>summis</u> <u>festivitatibus</u>   5
    Tr87 94'95

<u>Kyrie</u> <u>pascale</u>   5
    Ao 23'; MuEm 34'35; Tr90 75-75'; Tr92 24; Tr93 106-106'

Kyrie pater cuncta   5
    Ao 21'22; Ao 56'; Tr92 130; Tr93 120; Tr93 125'

Et in terra   1
    Tr92 120'121

Et in terra ad modum tube   1
    BL 180; Ao 95'96; Tr90 131'132; Tr93 161'162

Et in terra   2
    BL 192; Tr87 15'16'; Tr88 384'386; Ca6 31'33; Ca11 14-15

Et in terra in Dominicis   5
    Tr92 91'92

Et in terra in galli cantu   5
    BL 171; Tr92 149'150

Et in terra spiritus et alme   5
    BL 170; MuEm 57'58'; Tr90 151-152; Tr92 65-66; Tr93 182-183

Et in terra   6
    Tr92 144'146'

Et in terra de quaremiaulx   6
    BL 190

Et in terra   2[b]
    MuEm 97'98

Et in terra (contra voice by Dufay)   2[a]
    Ca6 24'27; Ca11 15'18

MOTETS

Alma redemptoris mater   2
    BL 257; BU 64-65

Alma redemptoris mater   2[b]
    Tr92 178'179; ModB 57'58

Anima mea   2[b]
    BL 265; Ox 27'28; Tr87 157'158

Apostolo glorioso   2
    BL 267

Ave regina celorum   2[b]
    BL 258; Ven 29'30; Ox 62; Tr87 154'; PC 61'

Ave regina celorum   8
    Tr88 327'329; ModB 59'60; MuEm 77'78

Ave regina celorum   9
    SPB90 25'27

Ave virgo que de celis   1
    Tr92 35'36; MuEm 109'110

Balsamus et munda   3
    BL 204-205

Ecclesie militantis   3
    Tr87 95'96, 85'86

Fulgens iubar   6
    ModB 121'123

Flos florum   1
    BL 264; Ox 25'26; ModB 56'57

Gaude virgo 2^b
    BL 227-228; MuEm 5'7

Inclita stella 2^b
    BL 208

Juvenis qui puellam   6
    MuL 14'15'

Magnanime gentis   6
    ModB 63'64

Mirandas parit   8
    Tr88 24'26; ModB 62'63

Moribus et genere   8
    ModB 74'76

Nuper rosarum   6
    Tr92 21'23; ModB 67'68'

O beate Sebastiane   4
    BL 311; ModB 58'59

O gemma lux   2
    BL 289; Ox 130'131

O gloriose tyro   8
    ModB 65'66

O proles yspanie   6
    Tr87 113'115; Tr88 207'209; ModB 60'62

O sancte Sebastiane   3
    BL 244; Ox 31'32

O tres piteulx   8
    MC 152'151; Ricc 34'36

Rite maiorem   3
    BL 209

Salve flos   6
    ModB 64'65

Salve regina   8
    Tr88 349'352; Mon 2 86'88

Si quereris miracula   6
    Tr87 115'117

Supremum est mortalibus   4
    BL 203; BU 56-57; Tr92 32'34; ModB 66'67; MuEm 107'109

Vasilissa ergo   1
    BL 273; Ox 132'133; Tr87 57'58

Erroneously Ascribed to Dufay

Qui latuit   3
    Tr87 109; MuEm 1

Veni dilecti   7
    BL 301^b; Tr87 125'; Ao 206'

Anonymous, Ascribed to Dufay

Elizabeth Zacharie   4
    Tr87 158'160

O sidus yspanie   8
    Tr88 205'207

BRIEF LITURGICAL PIECES

(The eleven proper cylces of Tr88 attributed to Dufay by Feininger are not listed here, but are discussed in Chapter 8.)

Alleluias

Alleluia veni sancte spiritus   8
    Tr88 117'118; Tr90 420

Antiphons

Hic vir despiciens   8
    ModB 50'

Magi videntes   8
    ModB 55

O gemma martirum   8
    ModB 49'

Petrus apostolus   8
    ModB 51

Propter nimiam 8
  ModB 52'

Salve nos Domine 8
  Tr90 288

Salve sancte pater 8
  ModB 50

Sapiente filio pater 8
  ModB 50'

Benedicamus Domino

Benedicamus Domino 7
  BL 169^b; ModB 29'

Benedicamus Domino 7
  BL 114; Tr87 57; Tr90 459'460; ModB 29

Hymns

Ad cenam agni 7
  Tr89 377'; ModB 7'8; RS 15 23'24

Audi benigne 7
  ModB 5'; RS 15 15'16; Ca32 157'; MC 26'

Aurea luce 5
  BL 320^b; ModB 13'14; SPB80 186; RS 15 39'40, 41'42

Aures ad nostram 8
  ModB 6; RS 15 18'19

Ave maris stella 5
  BL 318; BU 25; ModB 4'5; RS 15 42'43; MuEm 81'; Tr92 236'

Conditor alme siderum 5
  BL 311^b; Tr92 61; ModB 1; RS 15 4'; MuEm 85'

Criste redemptor 5
  BL 313; Tr92 134; ModB 1'2; SPB80 182; RS 15 5'6; MC 26'

Criste redemptor 5
  BL 318^b

Criste redemptor 7
  BL 319; Tr90 1; Tr92 96; Tr92 237, ModB 15'16;
    RS 15 7'8; RS 15 50'51; MC 41'

Deus tuorum 5
  BL 321^b; ModB 19'; SPB80 187'; RS 15 56'57; BL 323^b;
    ModB 20';

Exultet celum   5
    BL 321; ModB 17'18; SPB80 189'; RS 15 53'54, 55'56;
        MuEm 71; MuEm 73; FM112 11

Exultet celum (contratenor by Dufay)   9
    PrS 278

Festum nunc celebre   7
    Tr87 166'; MuEm 151'152

Hostis Herodes   5
    BL 313^b; Tr92 238'; ModB 2'3. 3'4; Ao 219; RS 15 9'10

Iste confessor   5
    BL 322^b; Tr92 238; ModB 20; RS 15 62'64

Jhesu nostra redempcio   5
    BL 314^b; ModB 8'9

O lux beata   5
    BL 315^b; Tr92 14; ModB 11'12; SPB80 184'; RS 15 32'33,
        MC 32

Pange lingue   5
    BL 316^b; Tr92 238'239; ModB 10'11; RS 15 34'35; Tr92 236

Proles de celo   8
    ModB 21-20'

Sanctorum meritis   5
    BL 322; Tr92 237'; ModB 18'19; RS 15 58'59

Tibi Criste splendor   5
    BL 319^b

Urbs beata   5
    BL 317^b; ModB 14'15; RS 15 68'70

Ut queant laxis   5
    BL 320; Tr92 239'; ModB 12'13; RS 15 37'38

Veni creator spiritus   5
    BL 315; Tr92 30; Tr93 357'; ModB 9'10; SPB80 184;
        MuEm 55; RS 15 29'30; FM112 5'6; MC 30

Vexilla regis   6
    Tr92 72; ModB 6-7'; RS 15 20'21; Ca32 258'; MC 27

                              Magnificats

Magnificat primi toni   8^a
    ModB 31-32'; SPB80 196'198; FM112 13'15

Magnificat <u>tertii</u> <u>toni</u>   8^b
    Tr89 165-165'; Mil 3 8'10; MC 42'44; RS 15 95'99;
      SPB80 200'203

Magnificat <u>quinti</u> <u>toni</u>   5
    ModB 43'44'; SPB80 203'205

Magnificat <u>sexti</u> <u>toni</u>   8
    Tr90 330'331; Tr92 17'18; BL 198; ModB 37-38';
      SPB80 207'209; MuEm 138'139; FM112 17'21; Tr92 19'21

Magnificat <u>octavi</u> <u>toni</u>   6
    Tr92 9'11; ModB 39'40'; SPB80 211'213; FM112 21'22

Sequences

<u>In</u> <u>epiphaniam</u> <u>Domino</u>   5
    Tr87 63'65

<u>Isti</u> <u>sunt</u> <u>due</u> <u>olive</u>   5
    Tr87 61'63

<u>Lauda</u> <u>syon</u>   5
    Tr92 98'100'; Tr93 230'232; MuEm 67'69

*<u>Letabundus</u> <u>exultet</u>   1
    Tr92 68'69

<u>Letabundus</u> <u>exultet</u>   5
    BL 324-325; Tr92 66'67

*<u>Mittit</u> <u>ad</u> <u>virginem</u>   5
    BL 336-337; Tr92 67'68'

<u>Rex</u> <u>omnipotens</u>   5
    Tr87 65'67'

*<u>Sancti</u> <u>spiritus</u> <u>assit</u>   5
    Tr92 36'37'

<u>Beni</u> <u>sancte</u> <u>spiritus</u>   5
    BL 325^b 326; Ao 185'186; MuEm 88'89

<u>Veni</u> <u>sancte</u> <u>spiritus</u>   5
    Tr92 100'101

<u>Victime</u> <u>pascale</u> <u>laudes</u>   5
    Tr92 23'24; MuEm 59'

*   Anonymous, attributed to Dufay by me

SECULAR WORKS

Adieu ce bons vins   2[b]
  Ox 140

Adieu m'amour   8
  Porto 70'71; MC 3

Adieu quitte le demeurant   7
  Tr90 303

Belle plaissant   2[a]
  Ox 91'

Belle que vous   1
  Tr87 136'

Belle vueilles moy vengier   8
  FM176 38'40; MC 4'5

Belle vueillies moy retenir   3
  Ox 50'

Belle vueillies vostre mercy   4
  Ox 118'119; BU 110; PC 43

Bien doy servir   7
  Tr87 153'154

Bien veignes vous   2[b]
  Ox 34'

Bon jour bon mois   2[b]
  Ox 44'; MuEm 23'; PC 52'53, 64

Ce jour de l'an   1
  Ox 17

Ce jour le doibt   7
  Ox 79; Tr87 137'; Vienna 5094 148'

Ce moys de may   2[a]
  Ox 17'; PR 103'104

C'est bien raison   4
  Ox 55'55

Craindre vous vueil   7
  Ox 5; Tr90 365; MuEm 54'; EscA 12'13

De ma haulte   9
  Ricc 17'18

De partes vous male bouche   8[b]
  MC 12'; BQ 16 25'26

Dieu gard la bone 8^b
FM176 24'25; Sev 91'92; Glo 180

Dona gentile bella 7
Mel 43'44; Pav 52'53; PRo 2'3

Dona i ardenti ray 2^b
Ox 73

Donnez l'assault 7
Tr87 119'120; Mel 71'72; Tr93 364'365

Du tout m'estoie 9
Pix 123'124; FM59 25'26; FM176 9'11;
Ricc2 69'70

En languir en piteux 7
Tr92 227'226

Entre les plus plaines 7
Porto 73'74

Entre vous 1
Ox 34'

Estrines moy 2^b
Ox 20'21; EscA 59'60

Franc cuer gentile 9
Tr92 180; EscB 20'21; Bux 62'63; Tr93 371'372

He compaignons 2^b
Ox 34; MuL

Helas et quant vous 1
PR 89'90

Helas ma dame 2^a
Ox 33'

Helas mon dueil 9
Porto 74'76

Invidia inimica 1
Ox 128'129; BU 102-103; FP 17'18

J'atendray tant 2^a
Ox 51

J'ay grant desir 2^a
P 4917 15'16

J'ay mis mon cuer 1
Ox 126

Je donne a tous 1
Ox 77; MuEm 52

Je me complains 2^a
   Ox 18

Je nay deubta fors   7
   Tr87 136'137

Je ne puis plus 2^b
   Ox 55'

Je ne suy plus 2^a
   Ox 52; Tr87 136; PR 97; PC 61'

Je ne vis oncques   9
   Lab 42'43; Wolf 38'39; PRo 60'62; MC 29'; MC 150; Tr90 352';
     FM176 50'51; P 4 40'41; Mn 94'95; Niv 51'52; Ricc2 72'73

Je prens congie   7
   PR 109'110

Je requier a tous   1
   Ox 67

Je triumph de crudel dueil   9
   Porto 76'77

Je veul chanter   1
   Ox 33'; PR 102'

Je vous pri 8^a
   FM178 74'75; FM107 14'15; MC 160; EscB 120'121; Pix 26'27;
     Ricc 2 67'68
La belle se siet 2^a
   Ox 31; BU 104; PR 108'109; PC 61

La dolce vista 2^a
   RU 11'12

L'alta belleza   1
   Ox 40'

Las que feray   7
   Ox 72; EscA 56'57; Str 90

Les doleurs   9
   Dij 133'134; Niv 60'61

Le serviteur   9
   PC 25'26; MC 103 (p. 347); BerK 4'5; Dij 92'93; EscB 76'77;
     Cord 33'34; Ricc 22'23; Pav 40'41; Per 67'68; Porto 64'65;
     C.G. 84'85; Tr90 358'359; Wolf 24'25; PRo 33'34;
     FM59 277'278; Bl09 84'85; Bux 3'; Bux 122'

Ma belle dame je vous pri   1
   Ox 139'

Ma belle dame souverainne 2^a
   Ox 140'

Malheureulx cuer   9
    Lab 25'27; Wolf 25'27; Mn 101'103

Ma plus mignonne   8^a
    Niv 64'65

Mille bonjours   7
    EscB 26'27; Str 114, 143; Bux 67'; MuEm 86; PC74'75

Mon bien m'amour   7
    Tr87 135'

Mon chier amy   2
    Ox 134'

Mon cuer me fait   1
    Ox 19'20

Mon seul plaisir   9
    Lab 65'66; Wolf 41'43; FM176 58'59; Porto 59'60; EscB 27'28;
        PC 23'24; Ricc2 48'49; PRo 44'46; Pix 69'70; Pav 24'25;
        BerK 20'21; Mn 22'23; PC 3'

Navre je suy   1
    Ox 78'; MuEm 96; PR98

Ne je ne dors   8
    FM176 29'30

Or pleust a Dieu   7
    Ox 71'; EscA 23'24

Par droit je puis   1
    BL 260^b; Ox 18'19

Par le regart   7
    Mel 73'74; Lab 66'67; Wolf 36'37; Porto 61'62; Sev 49';
        PC 21; MC 10'; EscB 40'41; Pav 47'48; Pix 39'40;
        BerK 13'14; Tr93 318'

Passato e il tempo   1
    Ox 134

Portugaler   2^b
    MuEm 65; MuEm 77; Str 92'93; MuEm 92'; Bux 21—21'

Pour ce que veoir   1
    Ox 18'

Pour l'amour   2^b
    Ox 135'136; MuEm 131'132

Pouray je avoir   7
    Ox 80; EscA 24'25; PR 97'; Str 129

Puisque celle qui me tient   7
    Tr87 134'

Puis que vous estez campieur   8^a
    Dij 99'100; Niv 15'16

Quel fronte signorille   2^b
    Ox 73

Qu'est devenue   7
    Porto 72'73

Resistera   9
    FM176 130'132

Resveillies vous   1
    Ox 126'

Resvelons vous   1
    Ox 34'

Se la face   7
    Ox 53'54; Tr89 424'425; Pav 65'66; RU 9'10; EscB 135'136;
        Str 128; Wolf 40'41; Mn 69'70; Lab 64'65; Bux 83, 255

Se ma damme   1
    Ox 66'; PR112'

Seigneur Leon   7
    Pix 27'28; Ricc2 68'69; BerK 5'6; Vienna 5094 154'155

S'il est plaisir   8
    MuEm 82'83

Trop lonc temps   7
    RU 14'15

Va ten mon cuer   7
    Porto 60'61; BerK 19'20

Vergene bella   4
    BL 234; BU 70'71; Ox 133'134

Vo regart et doulche maniere   7
    MuEm 65'66; MuEm 82

Vostre bruit   9
    Mel 22'23; PRo 28'29; Tr89 415'416; FM176 36'38; PC 20';
        Lab 22'23; CG 85'86; Glo 273

APPENDIX B

Manuscript Abbreviations

Ao	Aosta, Seminario, ms. without signature
BerK	Berlin, Kupferstichkabinett 78 C. 28
BL	Bologna, Liceo musicale, Q 15 (olim 37)
Br5557	Brussels, Bibliothèque royale de Belgique, ms. 5557
BQ 16	Bologna, Liceo musicale, Q 16
BU	Bologna, Bibl. Universitaria, 2216
Bux	Munich, Staatsbibl., Cim. 352b (= mus. 3725)
Ca6	Cambrai, Bibl. de la ville, ms. 6
Ca11	Cambrai, Bibl. de la ville, ms. 11
Ca32	Cambrai, Bibl. de la ville, ms. 32
CG	Città del Vaticano, Cappella Giulia, cod. XIII, 27
Cov	The Coventry Corporation, ms. A3
Dij	Dijon, Bibliothèque Publique, ms. 517
EscA	Escorial, Monasterio, V. III. 24
EscB	Escorial, Bibl., ms. a. IV. 24
FM59	Florence, Bibl. naz. Magliab., XIX, 59
FM107	Florence, Bibl. naz. Magliab., XIX, 107 bis
FM112	Florence, Bibl. naz. Magliab., XIX, 112 bis
FM176	Florence, Bibl. naz. Magliab., XIX, 176
FM178	Florence, Bibl. naz. Magliab., XIX, 178
FP	Florence, Bibl. naz., Panciatichiano 26
Lab	Laborde Chansonnier, Library of Congress, Washington, D.C.
MC	Monte Cassino, Monasterio 871 N
Mel	Mellon Chansonnier, Yale University Library, New Haven, Conn.
Mil3	Milan, Fabbrica del Duomo, cod. 2267
Mn	Munich, Staatsbibl., mus. 3232 (olim germ. cgm. 810)
ModB	Modena, Bibl. Estense, lat. 471 (α X, I, II)
ModE	Modena, Bibl. Estense, cod. lat. 456
Mon 2	Munich, Staatsbibl., mus. 3154
MuEm	Munich, Staatsbibl., mus. 3232a (lat. 14274)
MuL	Munich, Staatsbibl., mus 3224
Niv	Paris, Bibl. G. Thibaut, Chansonnier Nivelle de la Chaussée
Ox	Oxford, Bodleian Library, Canonici misc. 213
OH	Old Hall, St. Edmund's College, Old Hall Manuscript
Pav	Pavia, Bibl. Universitaria, Aldini 362

PC	Paris, Bibl. nationale, nouv. acq. franc. 4379
Pix	Paris, Bibl. nat., fr. 15123
Porto	Porto, Bibl. Communal 714
PR	Paris, Bibl. nat., nouv. acq. franc. 6771
PRo	Paris, Bibl. nat., Chansonnier Rothschild (Cordiforme)
PrS	Prague, Strahov Monastery, D. G. IV. 47
P 4	Paris, Bibl. nat., fonds franc., ms. 1597
P4917	Paris, Bibl. nat., fonds franc., nouv. acq. 4917
Ricc	Florence, Bibl. Ricc. 2794
Ricc2	Florence, Bibl. Ricc. 2356
RS14	Rome, Bibl. Vaticana, Cappella Sistina, ms. 14
RS15	Rome, Bibl. Vaticana, Cappella Sistina, ms. 15
RS49	Rome, Bibl. Vaticana, Cappella Sistina, ms. 49
RU	Rome, Bibl. Vaticana, urb. lat. 1411
Sc	Edinburgh, National Library of Scotland, Adv. ms. 5-1-15
Sev	Seville, Bibl. Côlombina, cod. 5-1-43
Str	Strasbourg, Bibl. de la ville, M.222 C.22
SPB80	Rome, San Pietro B80
Tr87-92	Trent, Castello del Buon Consiglio, mss. 87-92
Tr93	Trent, Archivio Capitolare, 93
Ven	Venice, Bibl. Marciana, ms. ital., IX, 145
Wolf	Wolfenbüttel. Herzog-August Bibl., ms. extravag. 287

B109	Bologna, Liceo musicale, ms. 109
Co 17	Copenhagen, Kongelige Bibl., ms. fragment 17
Glo	Berlin, Staatsbibl., Mus. ms. 40098 (olim Z. 98)
Vienna 5094	Vienna, Nationalbibl., Cod. 5094

BIBLIOGRAPHY

Adler, Guido, and others, "Sechs Trienter Codices. Erste Auswahl," Denkmäler der Tonkunst in Österreich, VII, Vienna, 1900.

_____, "Zweite Auswahl," DTO, XI/1, 1904.

_____, "Dritte Auswahl," DTO, XIX/1, 1912.

_____, "Vierte Auswahl," DTO, XXVII/1, 1920.

_____, "Fünfte Auswahl," DTO, XXXI, 1924.

_____, "Sechste Auswahl," DTO, XL, 1933.

Apel, Willi, The Notation of Polyphonic Music 900-1600, 4th edition, Cambridge, 1953.

Apfel, Ernst, "Über den vierstimmigen Satz im 14. und 15. Jahrhundert," AfMW 18, 1961, pp. 34-51.

Auda, A. "La Prolation dans l'edition princeps de la Messe 'L'Homme Arme' de Palestrina et sa Resolution dans l'edition de 1599," Scriptorium 2, 1948, pp. 85-102.

_____, "Le Tactus Clef de la Paléographie Musicale des XVe et XVIe siècles," Scriptorium 2, 1948, pp. 44-66.

_____, "Le Tactus principe générateur de l'interprétation de la musique polyphonique classique," Scriptorium 4, 1950, pp. 44-66.

_____, "La transcription en notation moderne de 'Liber Missarum' de Pierre de la Rue," Scriptorium 1, 1946, pp. 119-128.

Becherini, Bianca, "Due canzoni de Dufay del Codice Fiorentino 2794," La Bibliofilia 43, 1941, pp. 124-135.

Besseler, Heinrich, Bourdon und Fauxbourdon, Leipzig, 1950.

_____, (ed.), Capella, Kassel & Basel, 1950-51.

_____, "Dufay," Die Musik in Geschichte und Gegenwart 3, 1954, pp. 889-912.

_____, "Dufay in Rom," AfMW.15, 1958, pp. 1-19.

_____, (ed.), "Guillaume Dufay: Zwölf geistliche und weltliche Werke," Das Chorwerk 19, 1932.

_____, "The Manuscript Bologna Biblioteca Universitaria 2216," MD 6, 1952, pp. 39-65.

_____, Die Musik des Mittelalters und der Renaissance, Potsdam, 1931.

_____, "Neue Dokuments zum Leben und Schaffen Dufays," AfMW 9, 1952. pp. 159-176.

_____, "Studien zur Musik des Mittelalters II," AfMW 8, 1927, pp. 137-258.

Bockholdt, Rudolf, Die Frühen Messenkompositionen von Guillaume Dufay,
        Tutzing, 1960.

Boepple, Paul, (ed.), Guillaume Dufay: Magnificat, New York, 1945.

Borren, Charles van den, Études sur le XVe siècle musical, Antwerp, 1941.

_____, Guillaume Dufay, Brussels, 1925.

_____, Le ms. musical M.222 C.22 de la Bibl. de Strasbourg, Antwerp, 1924.

_____, (ed.), Pièces polyphoniques profanes de provenance liégeoise,
        Brussels, 1950.

_____, (ed.), Polyphonia Sacra, London, 1932.

Bukofzer, Manfred, "Caput Redivivum: a New Source for Dufay's Missa Caput,"
        JAMS 4, 1951, pp. 97-110.

_____, (ed.), John Dunstable: Complete Works, London, 1953 (Musica Britan-
        nica, VIII).

_____, Studies in Medieval and Renaissance Music, New York, 1950.

_____, "Changing Aspects of Medieval and Renaissance Music," MQ 44, 1958,
        pp. 15-16.

Clercx, Suzanne, "Aux origines du faux-bourdon," RdM 40, 1957, pp. 151-165.

_____, Johannes Ciconia, un musicien liégeois et son temps (vers 1335-1411),
        Brussels, 1960.

Coussemaker, E. (ed.), Scriptorum de musica medii aevi, Paris, 1864-1876.

Dart, Thurston, "A Footnote for Morley's 'Plain and Easy Introduction,'"
        M & L 35, 1954, p. 183.

Dèzes, Karl, "Das Dufay zugeschriebene Salve Regina eine deutsche Kompo-
        sition," ZfMW 10, 1927, pp. 327-362.

_____, "Der Mensuralcodex des Benediktinerklosters Sancti Emmerami zu
        Regensburg," ZfMW 10, 1927, pp. 65-105.

_____, "Van den Borren's 'Dufay,'" ZfMW 9, 1926, pp. 294-307.

Dahlhaus, Carl, "Zur Theorie des Tactus im 16. Jahrhundert," AfMW 17, 1960,
        pp. 22-39.

Feininger, Laurence, (ed.), Documenta Polyphoniae Liturgicae Sanctae Eccle-
        siae Romanae, Rome, 1947-52, I, pp. 1-4, 7, 9, 10.

_____, (ed.) Monumenta Polyphoniae Liturgicae Sanctae Ecclesiae Romanae,
        Rome, 1948-52, I & II, pp. 1, 2, 4.

Gerber, Rudolf, (ed.), "Guillaume Dufay: Sämtliche Hymen," Das Chorwerk 49,
        1937.

Gerbert, Martin, (ed.), Scriptores ecclesiastici de musica sacra potissimum,
        3 vols., 1784.

Goldthwaite, Scott, "Rhythmic Pattern Signposts in the 15th-Century Chanson,"
        JAMS 11, 1958, pp. 177-188.

Gombosi, Otto, Jacob Obrecht: Eine stilkritische Studie, Leipzig, 1925.

Günther, Ursula, "Der Gebrauch des tempus perfectum diminutum in der Hands-
        schrift Chantilly 1047," AfMW 17, 1960, pp. 277-297.

_____, "Die Anwendung der Diminution in der Handschrift Chantilly 1047," AfMW
        17, 1960, pp. 1-21.

Haberl, Fr. X. Bibliographischer und Thematischer Musik-Katalog des päpst-
        lichen Kapellarchives, Leipzig, 1888.

_____, "Die römische 'schola cantorum' und die päpstlichen Kapellsänger bis zur Mitte des 16. Jahrhunderts," VfMW 3, 1887, pp. 189-296.

_____, "Wilhelm du Fay. Monographische Studie über dessen Leben und Werke," VfMW 1, 1885, pp. 397-530.

Hamm, Charles, "A Group of Anonymous English Pieces in Trent 87," M & L 41, 1960, pp. 211-215.

_____, "Dating a Group of Dufay Works," JAMS 15, 1962, pp. 65-71.

_____, "Manuscript Structure in the Dufay Era," Acta 34, 1962, pp. 166-184.

_____, "The Manuscript San Pietro B80," RB 14, 1960, pp. 40-55.

Hannas, Ruth, "Concerning Deletions in the Polyphonic Mass Credo," JAMS 5, 1952, pp. 155-186.

Harrison, Frank L. Music in Medieval Britain, London, 1958.

Houdoy, J. Histoire artistique de la Cathédrale de Cambrai, Paris, 1880.

Jeppesen, Knud, Der Kopenhagener Chansonnier, Kopenhagen, 1927.

Kenney, Sylvia, "Contrafacta in the Works of Walter Frye," JAMS 8, 1955, pp. 182-202.

_____, "Origins and Chronology of the Brussels Manuscript 5557 in the Bibliothèque Royale de Belgique," RB 6, 1952, pp. 75-100.

Lerner, Edward, "The Polyphonic Magnificat in 15th-Century Italy," MQ 49, 1964, pp. 44-58.

Linderburg, Cornelius, (ed.), Johannes Regis: Opera Omnia, American Institute of Musicology, Rome, 1956 - .

Marix, Jeanne, Hostoire de la musique et des musiciens de la cour de Bourgogne, Strasbourg, 1939.

_____, Les musiciens de la cour de Bourgogne au XVe siècle, Paris, 1937.

Morley, Thomas, A Plain and Easy Introduction to Practical Music (1597), ed. by R. Alec Harman, London, 1952.

Parrish, Carl, The Notation of Medieval Music, New York, 1957.

Pirro, André, Histoire de la musique de la fin du XIVe siècle à la fin du XVIe, Paris, 1940.

Plamenac, Dragan, (ed.), Johannes Ockeghem: Sämtliche Werke I, Leipzig, 1927.

_____, (ed.), Johannes Ockeghem: Collected Works II, New York, 1947.

_____, "A Reconstruction of the French Chansonnier in the Biblioteca Colombina, Seville," MQ 37, 1951, pp. 501ff.; MQ 38, 1952, pp. 85ff. and 245ff.

_____, "A Postscript to 'The "Second" Chansonnier of the Biblioteca Riccardiana,'" AM 4, 1956, pp. 261-265.

_____, "An Unknown Composition by Dufay?" MQ 40, 1954, pp. 190-200.

_____, "Browsing Through a Little-Known Manuscript," JAMS 13, 1960, pp. 102-111.

_____, "The 'Second' Chansonnier of the Biblioteca Riccardiana," AM 2, 1954, pp. 128-169.

Praetorius, Ernst, Die Mensuraltheorie des Franchinus Gafurius und der fol-
     genden Zeit bis zur Mitte des 16. Jahrhunderts, Leipzig, 1905.

Ramsbotham, A., Collins, H. B., and Hughes, Dom Anselm, The Old Hall Manu-
     script, 3 vols., London, 1933-38.

Reaney, Gilbert, (ed.), Early Fifteenth-Century Music, American Institute
     of Musicology, 1955.

_____, "The Manuscript Oxford, Bodleian Library, Canonici Misc. 213," MD 9,
     1955, pp. 73-104.

Rehm, Wolfgang, (ed.), Gilles Binchois: Chansons, Mainz, 1957.

Reese, Gustave, Music in the Renaissance, New York, 1954.

Sachs, Curt, Rhythm and Tempo, New York, 1953.

Schünemann, Georg, "Zur Frage des Taktschlagens und der Textbehandlung in
     der Mensuralmusik," SIMG 10, 1908, pp. 73-114.

Seay, Albert, "The Proportionale Musices of Johannes Tinctoris," Journal of
     Music Theory 1, 1957, pp. 22-75.

Stainer, J.F.R., and Stainer, C. Dufay and his Contemporaries, London, 1898.

Stephan, Wolfgang, Die Burgundisch-Niederländische Motette zur Zeit Ockeg-
     hems, Kassel, 1937.

Stevens, Denis, "The Manuscript Edinburgh, National Library of Scotland,
     Adv. MS. 5.1.15," MD 13, 1959, pp. 167ff.

Strunk, Oliver, Source Readings in Music History, New York, 1950.

_____, Review of Documenta Polyphoniae Liturgicae S. Ecclesiae Romanae,
     Series 1 (1 & 2), JAMS 2, 1949, pp. 107-110.

Thibaut, G. "Quelques chansons de Dufay," RM 11, 1924, pp. 97-102.

Tirabassi, Antonio, Grammaire de la notation proportionnelle et sa trans-
     scription moderne, Brussels, 1928.

_____, La mesure dans la notation proportionnelle et sa transcription
     moderne, Brussels, 1927.

_____, "Sur quelques particularités séméiographiques des manuscrits musi-
     caux de la Bibliothèque Royale de Belgique," Scriptorium 1, 1946-47,
     pp. 156-158.

Trowell, Brian, "Some English Contemporaries of Dunstable," PRMA 1954-55,
     pp. 77-92.

Van, G. de, and Besseler, H. (ed.), Guglielmi Dufay: Opera Omnia, American
     Institute of Musicology, 1947-.

Van, G. de, "Inventory of Manuscript Bologna, Liceo Musicale, Q 15 (olim 37),"
     MD 2, 1948, pp. 231-257.

_____, "A Recently Discovered Source of Early Fifteenth Century Polyphonic
     Music," MD 2, 1948, pp. 5-74.

Wolf, Johannes, Geschichte der Mensural-Notation von 1250-1460, 3 vols.,
     Leipzig, 1904.

_____, Handbuch der Notationskunde, 2 vols., Leipzig, 1913-1919.

INDEX